INTERIOR SPACES DESIGNED BY ARCHITECTS

EDITED BY BARCLAY F. GORDON
ASSOCIATE EDITOR
ARCHITECTURAL RECORD

AN ARCHITECTURAL RECORD BOOK

McGraw-Hill Book Company

New York St. Louis San Francisco
Düsseldorf Johannesburg
Kuala Lumpur London Mexico
Montreal New Delhi Panama
Paris São Paulo Singapore
Sydney Tokyo Toronto

INTERIOR SPACES DESIGNED BY ARCHITECTS

The editors for this book were Jeremy Robinson and Hugh S. Donlan.
The designer was Jan V. White.

It was set in Optima by Norwalk Typographers, Inc., printed
by Halliday Lithograph Corporation, and bound by The Book Press.

234567890   HDBP   7654

Library of Congress Cataloging in Publication Data

Gordon, Barclay F   comp.
  Interior spaces designed by architects.

  A collection of photos. previously published in
Architectural record.
    1. Interior decoration.   2. Space (Architecture)
I. Architectural record.   II. Title.
NK2113.G67   729   73-21599

ISBN   0-07-002220-8

CIVIC AND COMMUNITY USE

TEACHING

WORSHIP

BUSINESS

SELLING AND DISPLAY

DINING AND DRINKING

THE PERFORMING ARTS

LIVING

FOREWORD

Rooted deep in the architect's training and self image is the conviction that he is a "problem solver" and also that *interior* and *exterior* are simply words used to describe opposite sides of the same wall. The design problems awaiting solution on both sides of the wall, he argues, are sometimes different but they are subject to the same kind of functional analysis and respond to the same rules of harmony and visual order. That, in simplified form, has been the essence of the "architectural interior" and the architect's justification for demanding a visual reconciliation between interior and exterior design.

Several factors have conspired in recent years to make this position less tenable. First, the gentle snowfall of new equipment and products became a blizzard. While the architect suspected a high degree of redundancy among these products, it was harder and harder just to keep track of them, much less test out their manufacturer's often extravagant claims for them. Second, during the boom years of the mid and late '60s, the continuing flow of commissions for new work tempted many an architect to relinquish his grip on projects sooner and leave their completion to a growing list of specialists who came in to place equipment, order furniture and specify interior finishes.

When the boom ended abruptly in 1969, and the flow of new work was choked down to a trickle, the architect's interest in interior design increased in a compensatory fashion. Not only did he have more time to carry design through to final completion and occupancy, but a higher proportion of his work was in the area of renovation, as school boards and other clients turned more and more to "found space." Many of the interiors in this collection are renovations. But whether new work or renovations, the architect's renewed commitment to interior design meant reorganizing his office procedures and extending his design capabilities. Most important, it meant updating his design vocabulary (the glass top table and the Barcelona chairs were no longer enough) and finding fresh images that suitably expressed the tempo and texture of contemporary life and values. That is an important part of what this book is about for the interior spaces shown here all date to the five year period between 1968 and 1973.

Many of them strive to express some of the ambiguous and discordant themes of modern life, the contradictions, the fast-moving images of television, films, and contemporary graphics. The use of highly reflective surfaces to produce distorted or even fractured images (see John Fowler's renovation of the Yale Freshman Commons, pages 158-159) is but one example. The widespread reliance on supergraphics, whether to convey information or simply to excite the senses (see Wendell Lovett's house, pages 214-216) has its parallel in the development of Op Art, Kinetic Art and even Psychedelic Art—and it seems to express some of the same quality of impermanence. One design mandate of the 1960s—to integrate mechanical equipment with building structure—is violated emphatically in many of these interiors where ductwork, pipe and even armored cable are not only exposed but treated as a primary feature of design.

The society's continually increasing mobility (soon to be arrested by the energy crisis and gasoline rationing?) has prolonged our interest in furniture that is demountable, stackable and portable although deflatable furniture has not had the market impact that many expected. A new direction in lighting design emerges in several of these interiors (see the Offices of ALCAN, pages 102-105) and the influence of Italian designers, well documented in New York's Museum of Modern Art's recent show entitled "The Italian Landscape", is also evident in this collection.

The reader who thumbs these pages will find other design messages aplenty—design messages that in combination will ultimately give the interiors of the '70s as distinctive a look as the interiors of the '30s. But more fundamental than the style it produces is the architect's basic approach to design. And as long as he continues to be a problem-solver, he will have a special place in the business of interior design and his work will merit serious study. This volume collects between its covers what we believe is the most varied and comprehensive group of architectural interiors published to date and gives these handsome spaces the study that their excellence has rightfully earned them.

INTERIORS FOR CIVIC AND

COMMUNITY USE

Most of the interiors in this section, despite their wide variety, were designed for state, city or local government agencies who represented the public client. The two city halls for Boston (page 14) and Scottsdale, Arizona (page 2) are very different in style and plan, but each is an affirmation of the belief that the democratic process is essentially open, or should be, and that a seat of government, whether monumental or vernacular in concept, should express openness and accessibility. Both of these interiors are carefully organized with good patterns of circulation and are also invested with a high level of design concern that makes each a source of pride to its community.

The Clinton Youth Center (page 24), the Kent Library (page 6) and the Permanente Clinic (page 22) are also buildings for community use with interiors that are designed with unusual sensitivity and skill. Of these, two are new and one is a renovation. The Clinton Youth Center by James Polshek & Associates is a remodelling of an old police precinct building into a small center for community services. The appearance of this kind of center in cities across the country marked the growing belief in the late '60s that the provision of youth and family services was an important tool in ameliorating those problems of urban life rooted in social and economic deprivation.

These buildings, and others like them, also indicate a return to the conviction that commissions for public buildings should be awarded on the basis of design competence rather than political connection. In many cases, this has meant design competitions, either national or regional and several buildings in this group are competition winners. But in whatever manner the architects have been selected, it is gratifying to see that many designers of ability are working again in the public sector for clients who range from city government to small community groups.

Neil Koppes

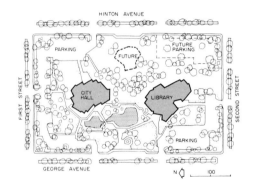

HINTON AVENUE

PARKING FUTURE FUTURE PARKING

CITY HALL LIBRARY

FIRST STREET SECOND STREET

PARKING

GEORGE AVENUE

N ◁ 100

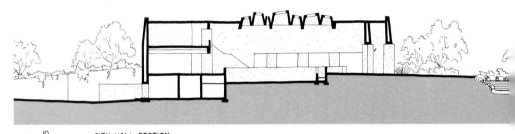

IO CITY HALL SECTION

A new civic center
for Scottsdale, Arizona
has fluid interiors
shaped by vernacular forms

Its forms, though, are not the only forces at work to give these spaces fluidity. The desert itself with its harsh glare and bright sun has shaped the building's exterior to a remarkable extent and the relaxed lifestyle of the Southwest accounts for much of the building's openness and informality.

When the cultural facility (see site plan) is completed in future, Scottsdale will have one of the most interesting and expressive civic groupings in any American city.

ENGINEERING PARKS & REC.

LOUNGE LOUNGE CONF

BUILDING INSPECTIONS COUNCIL

FINANCE

PLANNING CITY CLERK

CITY HALL N ◁ 20

The center is located in what had become a semi-blighted section of town, thanks to a meteoric rise in population —from 12,000 to nearly 70,-000—over the previous 10 years. Already, the new buildings and the park in which they are situated have revitalized the area, stimulating private as well as public development. Ultimately the master plan calls for developing the remainder of the 20-acre site assembled by the city, to provide facilities for such cultural activities as arts and crafts (an important part of Scottsdale), drama and music.

A CITY HALL THAT INVITES CITIZENS TO PARTICIPATE

The city hall is a building without interior partitions: everything and every process is open and accessible to the public. This is in keeping with the community's conviction that citizens should participate in the processes of their government and that the building which houses these processes should make it easy to do so. A remarkable procedure—the Scottsdale Town Enrichment Program (STEP)—involved some 400 residents, representing every section of the city, in providing direction for planning the center, and the buildings are, says Bennie Gonzales, the architect, a direct translation of STEP's beliefs. The heart of the concept is the use of the central lobby in each building as a community focus. In the city hall, the Council chamber occupies this space; in the library, the periodical lounge. In both buildings the space is sunk four feet below entrance level, with a low balustrade (for leaning by onlookers and overflow audience) surrounding it, and skylighting above through faceted colored glass. Departments to which the public needs ready access are on the main floor. Structure is load-bearing masonry, mortar washed. Slabs and roof beams are of prestressed concrete. Mechanical and electrical lines run in outer walls and in massive interior columns.

A LIBRARY WHOSE FACILITIES ARE ALL ACCESSIBLE

Similar in plan to the city hall, the library is equally open and inviting, reflecting the informal Southwestern way of life which the Council, in its brief charge to the architects, indicated was one of its criteria for the buildings' design. The central sunken space is used as a periodical lounge, with reading rooms and book shelves in the various reading rooms on the level above. The great central area has the dignity of monumental space but because of the angled direction of the massive columns, is also quite informal. All public services, as well as cataloging and processing, are located on the entrance level. Here, too, is a 100-seat auditorium, accessible from outside the building and from the lobby. On the mezzanine are administrative offices, staff lounge and board room, and a gallery currently used for art exhibitions but ready for expansion. The building was designed for a projected capacity of 125,000 volumes. The furnishings were selected by the architects and are not typical library furniture; some equipment was specially designed.

SCOTTSDALE CIVIC CENTER, Scottsdale, Arizona. Architects: *Gonzales Associates.* Engineers: *Foltz, Hamlyn & Adam, Inc.* (structural); *Richard E. Joachim & Associates* (mechanical); *William E. Meier & Associates* (electrical). Landscape architects: *Gonzales Associates.* General contractor: *Arnold Construction Company.*

LIBRARY SECTION   10

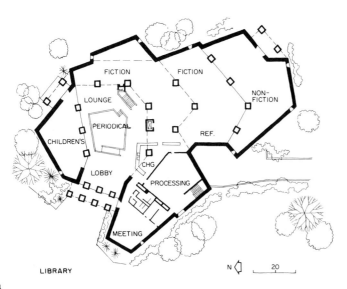

LIBRARY   N   20

Similarity in the exterior appearance of the city hall (pages 2-3) and the library, shown on this page and the next, is balanced off by the strong individuality of each building, influenced by their very different requirements. In the ultimate development of the 20-acre civic-cultural center site, the library will be a pivotal point.

Earth colors are used in the interiors of both city hall and library. Brown carpet contrasts with white textured walls and ceilings; wood furniture and colorful upholstery fabrics are lively accents. The total effect is of hand-crafted, non-commercial quality. Faceted colored glass skylights, are placed in the ceilings of both buildings to admit more warm colors in winter than in summer. The architects designed all interiors.

Warren Platner's design for a town library produces strong spaces and refined details

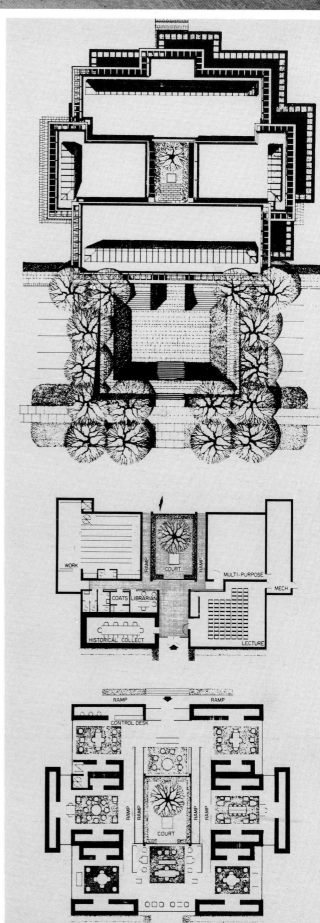

At Suffield, Connecticut, Warren Platner's design explores totally fresh ideas in library layout and, indeed, in the ways people like to use libraries; and for a budget of just over $800,000 gives the handsome town of Suffield, a new centerpiece of design excellence. This is Warren Platner's first completed building since he opened his own office; and it enhances his already established reputation as a designer of rare skills.

The library has two entrances. One (bottom in site plan, and photo at left) faces the village green. On this side, the visitor enters through a beautifully scaled, sunken, tree-enclosed terrace.

Directly through the doors (see lower level plan, at bottom), one first glimpses the handsome garden court that pours light directly into every part of the library and acts as a focus of the plan. Turning to either side of the court, the visitor ascends a gentle ramp which leads to the second level—where the other entrance (photo p. 8), the charge desk and catalog, and three general reading areas are located. These lower ramps can be closed by gates at their base, assuring single-point control of books when that is needed; but also permitting a lower-level auditorium, gallery, and rare book room to be used for evening meetings without librarian control.

This second-level, less formal entrance is, in fact, the most heavily used—for this side of the building is within a 30-second walk of the parking lot of a small but busy shopping center.

From this level, the ramps turn back on themselves along the interior court and slope up to the reference library. Halfway up these slopes are, to one side, the children's reading room; to the other, the music and art collection.

The plan (at right) of these upper levels begins to describe what is the most important and innovative feature of the design—the use of specially designed double-sided bookshelves to create book alcoves around all of the reading spaces. This design device, worth careful study by every library designer, is shown in the photos on the following pages.

KENT MEMORIAL LIBRARY, Suffield, Connecticut. Architects: *Warren Platner Associates Architects—associates of Warren Platner on this project: Jesse Lyons, Robert Brauer, and Frank Emery.* Engineers: *Pfisterer, Tor & Associates* (structural); *John L. Altieri* (mechanical/electrical). Consultants: *Jill Mitchell* (graphics); *Kenneth Shatter* (library). General contractor: *L B Construction Incorporated.*

A brick-paved system of ramps rising alongside the court permits easy use of book carts and gives complete access to the handicapped. The reading spaces (the reference room is at right) have no walls—all spaces are lined either with big panes of glass, or with books. To create these walls of books, to avoid reading spaces separate from book stack spaces, and to have enough space for 60,000 volumes, Platner created the alcoves seen—for example—at rear. These are formed by a shelf of books against the outer wall, with double-sided shelves set out from them. These reading spaces are, for a public building, small and intimate, with something of the feeling of a home library—yet they offer bold views to the outdoors and the garden court—and overlook all of the other reading areas. From inside, all is instantly understandable.

The book-alcove concept is seen clearly above, with double-sided shelves set out from single shelves along the exterior wall. The handsome lighting was devised simply by setting junction boxes at the corners of the forming pans before the roof was poured. The alcoves are lit by skylights under the perimeter roof monitors. Other photos show the auditorium, the rare books room, and the librarian's office. As usual, Platner's detailing is understated—and superb.

A megaspace with an adjustable ceiling system for this convention center in Denver

Currigan Hall is large—685 by 240 feet in size, with 100,000 square feet of clear-span exhibit space—but more impressive than its size are the simplicity of its concept and its quality of serenity. Structure and architecture work together to provide the required long-span space and to permit variations in scale, from the monumentality of the building itself to the 10 by 10 foot module of the individual display space. This concept, of huge building within which certain areas can be scaled down, won a statewide competition for a joint venture of three Denver architects, each of whom assumed specific responsibilities for the job: W. C. Muchow, administration and coordination; James T. Ream, design; Dayl Larson of Haller & Larson, production and supervision. The space frame which is so important a feature of the interior is also an essential part of the exterior, visible as the roof structure and as the support for the exterior walls which hang from it. As ceiling of the exhibition floor, it is visible from outside because of the "picket fence phenomenon" produced by the repetition of the slit windows at regular intervals along the exterior walls. To a viewer in motion, the walls appear transparent so that he sees the lacy frame as he moves past even though he is conscious of the walls as walls. The windows are tall narrow openings (18 inches by 30 feet) between the panels of weathering steel (10 by 30 feet) which make up the exterior wall. The light weight of the steel panels was important in their maintenance-free characteristic and their rich color. There are three floors: Basement with limited parking, some storage and mechanical equipment; main exhibition floor, and mezzanine which overhangs the sidewalk and straddles a street.

The space frame is the dominant feature of the building, architecturally and structurally, providing a surprisingly light (13.2 psf) and economical ($7 psf) roof system. The frame is a two-layer, three-dimensional system of inclined double Warren trusses, in which all members (24,000) are the same length (10 feet) and all joints (6,000) are a standard detail (but of special design: each is made up of three intersecting octagonal planes, accommodating up to 12 members). The 680 by 240 foot roof is in four sections, each 170 by 240 feet, supported by inverted pyramid columns which rest on five-foot-square concrete columns. The frame was assembled on the building floor section by section and raised in three phases, allowing, in the first phase, for attachment of the pyramid columns; in the second phase at 21 feet above floor, for placement of steel pipe columns at the four corners and pouring of concrete columns; and finally for positioning on these columns at the ultimate height of 46 feet above floor. Each section supports a massive mechanical penthouse containing transformers and cooling towers.

The key to the economic success of an exhibition-convention hall is its operating efficiency, particularly its provision for moving goods and people. Currigan Hall is exceptional in its handling of both. Trucks proceed from the street by ramp (there are two, one on each side of the building as photo at left shows) direct to the exhibit floor, unload under cover at any of 12 drive-in positions along one side or nine dock positions on the other. Loading and unloading (and even crate storage) is all horizontal, a considerable economy over vertical handling. People enter on foot across landscaped plazas or by car from the ramps. A mezzanine level with lounges, rest rooms, offices and control booths, provides a spectacular view of the space frame, pyramids and the vast floor with its space for 14,000.

MEZZANINE

OFFICES AND CONCESSIONS

EXHIBIT
UPPER PART HALL A
UPPER PART HALL B
EXHIBIT

OFFICES AND ESCALATORS

BRIDGE
DINING

AUDITORIUM

MAIN FLOOR

DRIVE-IN DOORS

LOBBY
HALL A
HALL B
LOBBY

LOADING DOCKS

50

LOWER FLOOR

RAMPS
RAMPS

LOBBY
EXHIBIT STORAGE
EXHIBIT STORAGE
LOBBY

MECHANICAL
MECHANICAL

The colorful pyramids that hang from the truss of the space frame are unique assets of Currigan Hall. They form an adjustable ceiling system (see reflected plan at right) designed to vary the scale of the vast interior by providing a canopy of suitable (and variable) height over each module of display space. Each pyramid contains lighting for special high intensity illumination. Pyramids can be lowered singly or in groups and, when not in use, nest in the grid of the space frame. The prismatic forms of these pyramids, and their colorful interior surfaces (red or yellow), seen against the web of the space frame, make "visual pageantry of the long perspective of the hall," to quote James Ream, partner in charge of design. The space frame, painted white, seems even lighter than it really is and the pattern of its thousands of members is a visual maze of extraordinary vitality. For daytime events, daylight from the slit windows adds to this sense of liveliness. The exhibition hall has been designed so that it can be divided at its mid point for smaller events; and the ceiling system can be adjusted to provide a lower over-all ceiling height.

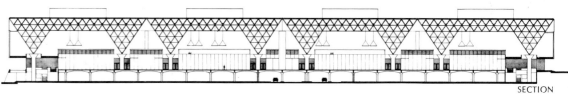

SECTION

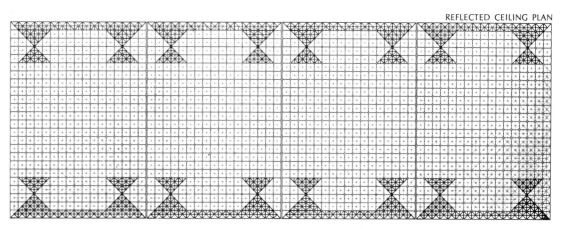

REFLECTED CEILING PLAN

Boston's new City Hall, already a landmark, emphasizes openness and accessibility within a powerful structural order

City Hall Square, comparable in scale to St. Mark's Square in Venice and St. Peter's Square in Rome, is essentially a trapezoid with two curved sides. The Boston City Hall architects, Kallmann, McKinnell & Knowles, have treated the square as a great brick plane on which people move—into and through the public spaces of City Hall, across to the raised podium of the Federal Office Building, or down by means of broad steps to Faneuil Hall (shown at the top of the site plan and in the photographs) and beyond to the old Quincy Market and the waterfront area. The south facade will face a secondary square which is to provide a setting for a new office building now complete and the Old State House (as shown in the drawing).

The projecting hooded elements (shown in the photograph right) mark the mayor's corner suite and the municipal library. This facade has been designed to eventually form an effective visual enclosure to Dock Square.

The basic volume within which the City Hall could be designed, and its specific location, had been determined in a master plan for the entire Government Center urban renewal area prepared for the Boston Redevelopment Authority by I. M. Pei Associates.

BOSTON CITY HALL, Boston. Client: *Government Center Commission of the City of Boston*—chairman: *Robert M. Morgan;* architects and engineers for the Boston City Hall: *a joint venture of Kallmann, McKinnell & Knowles, architects; Campbell, Aldrich & Nulty, architects; LeMessurier Associates, Inc., structural engineers*—project managers: *Robert C. Abrahamson, Henry A. Wood;* job captain: *Gordon F. Tully;* mechanical engineers: *Greenleaf Associates, H.V.A.C.; Cleverdon, Varney & Pike, electrical; Thompson Engineering Co., lighting consultant; Bolt, Beranek & Newman, acoustical consultant;* concrete technologist: *Herman G. Protze;* space planning: *Becker & Becker Associates;* furniture and graphics: *I.S.D., Inc.*—designer, *Louis Beal;* project manager: *Vida Stirbys;* graphic designer: *Carole Lipper;* general contractor: *J. W. Bateson Company.*

The spatial organization of Boston City Hall is highly complex. The site slopes downward and the first two floors within the brick mound are partially buried in the hill. The two lower floors (not shown) contain mechanical and computer spaces, central files, a garage and office space. The building's secondary entrance to the north is on the second floor, and from here the concourse moves upward by means of ramps and escalators to the third floor or mezzanine areas and to the principal entrance at the southwest corner. On the second and third floors are the services used by large numbers of citizens. The south entrance provides access to the ceremonial spaces—the mayor's suite, the council chamber, the councilmen's offices and the municipal reference library—all of which are suspended above the interior court. The court itself, on the fourth level, is an extension of City Square and is open to the sky and to all four exposures. The hooded projections in the photograph (left) express the council chamber and the councilmen's offices. The top floors contain office spaces requiring a minimum amount of public traffic.

The completed City Hall bears a very clear resemblance to the winning design because the space requirements, circulation and adjacency patterns prepared by the space planning firm of Becker & Becker and made part of the original competition program were quite thoroughgoing and realistic.

© Ezra Stoller (ESTO) photos

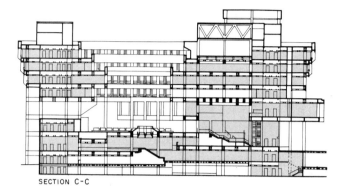

SECTION C-C

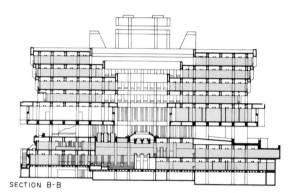

SECTION B-B

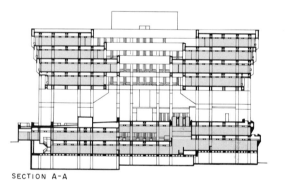

SECTION A-A

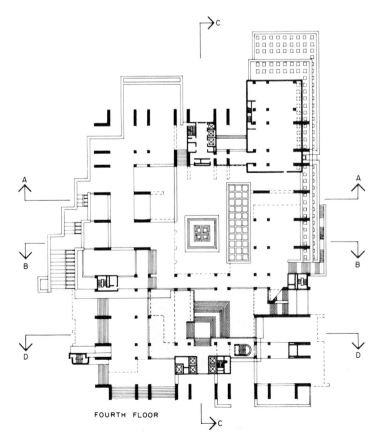

FOURTH FLOOR

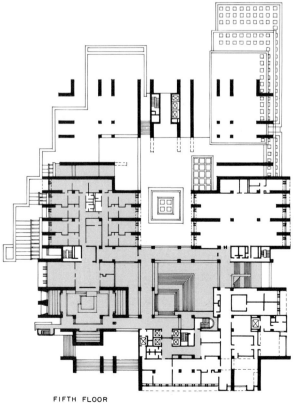

FIFTH FLOOR

15

The south entrance hall is the principal interior volume which links spatially all of the elements of the city government. Its light shafts (one of which is shown in the two pictures at right) extend upward to the full height of the building. The brick stair (shown below) is an extension of the brick-paved City Square, and takes the form of an amphitheater. From its upper level it offers views of Washington Street, the Old State House, Dock Square, Faneuil Hall, Quincy Market and the harbor beyond. It also gives access to the inner terrace and court (right) which is an elevated extension of the City Square and is linked to it and to Dock Square by ramps and stairs. The architects point out that the inner public court epitomizes the concept of openness and accessibility that generated the design of the City Hall. To be open day and night, it allows the citizen to walk through and be part of his City Hall without once opening a door.

Lili and Todor Gorchev

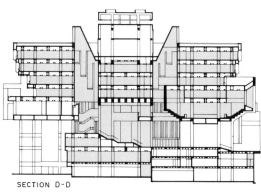

SECTION D-D

The concourse (shown below and at right) is entered from the north at a lower level. It provides generous lobby spaces interconnected by escalators, ramps and broad staircases for the 5000 persons who will do business there each day. Placing the most heavily used areas close to the ground in the building's brick-clad base has considerably reduced the number of elevators which the City Hall would otherwise require. The building will be newly furnished throughout. All movable furniture and built-ins have been designed or selected by ISD Incorporated, the interior design consultants. According to Louis Beal, executive vice president of ISD, the designers strove to select furnishings which could not be overpowered by the rugged monolithic character of the surroundings. At the same time, however, their choices were limited to furniture which could be obtained by publicly advertised competitive bid at prices which would be most advantageous to the city. Where possible stock or standard furnishings were used, and adapted where necessary to improve appearance and durability. Typical interiors include custom-built desks of which more than 1300 were made. The only major interior not to be designed by ISD will be the mayor's office (small photo). The new mayor, Kevin H. White, has elected to decorate his office in a traditional manner.

The structural system consists essentially of poured-in-place concrete columns and cores, precast concrete Vierendeel trusses, and precast non-structural members which carry the light fixtures and ducts. The structural bay is 14 ft-4 in. square with columns at 14 ft-4 in. or 28 ft-8 in. Modules are 4 ft-6 in. and 2 ft-8 in. General office floors have a clear height of 8 ft-6 in. below a structural depth of 5 ft. Mechanical equipment consists of a central modular duct system which passes horizontally through the truss openings and vertically at the cores. A perimeter induction unit system at the windows is fed vertically from the roof through precast exterior fins, as shown in the detail (opposite page right).

Lili and Todor Gorchev

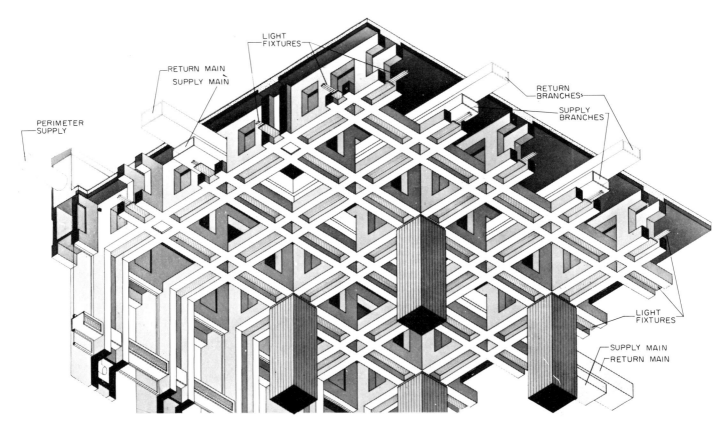

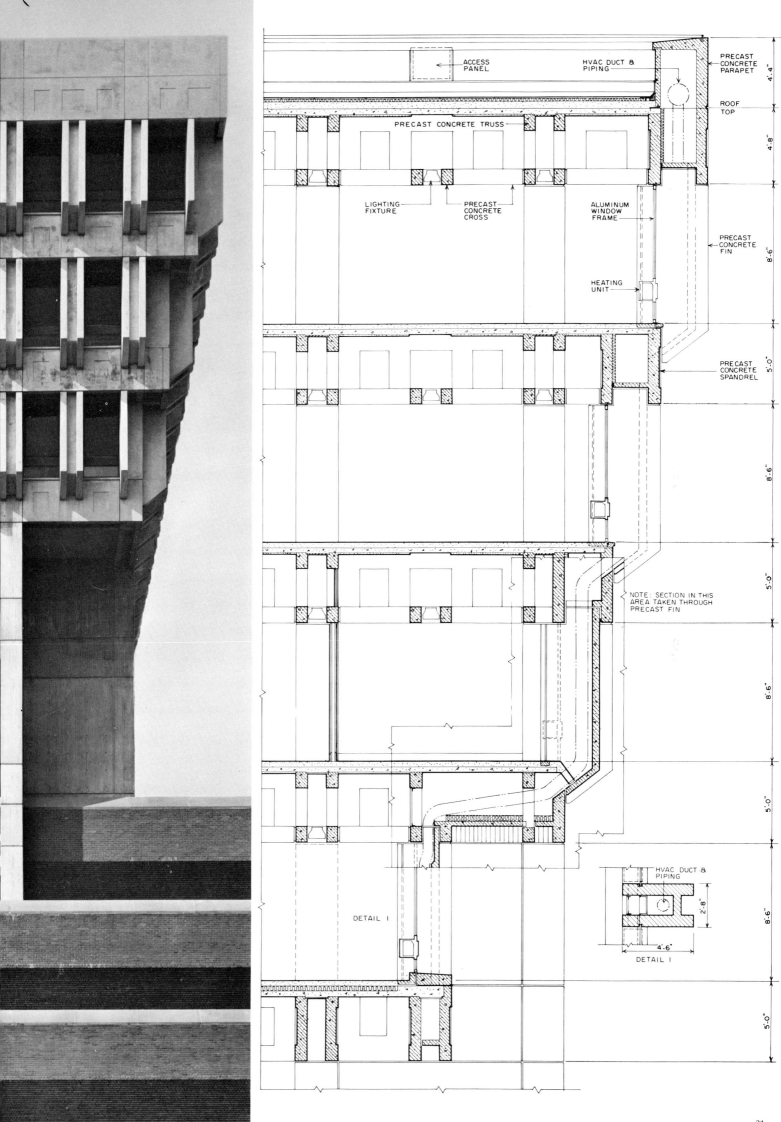

ACCESS
PANEL

HVAC DUCT &
PIPING

PRECAST
CONCRETE
PARAPET

4'-4"

PRECAST CONCRETE TRUSS

ROOF
TOP

4'-8"

LIGHTING
FIXTURE

PRECAST
CONCRETE
CROSS

ALUMINUM
WINDOW
FRAME

PRECAST
CONCRETE
FIN

8'-6"

HEATING
UNIT

PRECAST
CONCRETE
SPANDREL

5'-0"

8'-6"

NOTE: SECTION IN THIS
AREA TAKEN THROUGH
PRECAST FIN

5'-0"

8'-6"

DETAIL I

HVAC DUCT &
PIPING

2'-8"

4'-6"

DETAIL I

5'-0"

Art Hupy photos

A community health clinic centers on an interior court that is skylighted by a quarter-round clerestory

The concept of prepaid health care, especially when the plan is hospital-connected, has become increasingly attractive in the search for means to improve health care at reasonable cost. In California, Oregon and Hawaii, the Kaiser Foundation Health Plan operates a number of outpatient clinics of which this clinic in Beaverton, Oregon, is one. In connection with its clinics, though not necessarily adjacent to them, it also operates hospitals. Membership in the prepaid plan provides normal hospital care, with clinic visits and laboratory work at moderate additional charges. The Beaverton clinic serves a large suburban clientele and is connected wtih the Portland Kaiser Hospital. The clinic site is in a noisy, busy commercial area, and the building is designed to cut out as much of this hurly-burly as possible. The interior is designed around a large court, sky-lighted by a large half-dome which is a strong and dominant feature of the exterior. The resulting environment is both a pleasant and restful place for the clientele, and an efficient working environment for the staff. The organization of spaces and functions is based on prototype plans worked out by the architects and the client for similar facilities elsewhere. Examining rooms and doctors' offices are on two levels, with the entrance and certain support facilities at mid-level. The main circulation system for the public, both ambulatory and non-ambulatory, is the pair of ramps (one leading up to the second level, the other down to the lower level) which wind from mid-level through the interior court. Two sets of stairs and an elevator are also provided. The structure consists of reinforced concrete bearing walls, beams and slabs. The half-dome is post-tensioned. The interiors were designed by the architects.

THE PERMANENTE CLINIC, Beaverton, Oregon. Architects: *Wolff Zimmer Gunsul Frasca Ritter*. Engineers: *Stanley V. Carlson*, structural; *J. Donald Kroeker & Associates*, mechanical; *Grant Kelley & Associates*, electrical. Landscape architect: *Robert P. Perron*. General Contractor: *Henry M. Mason*.

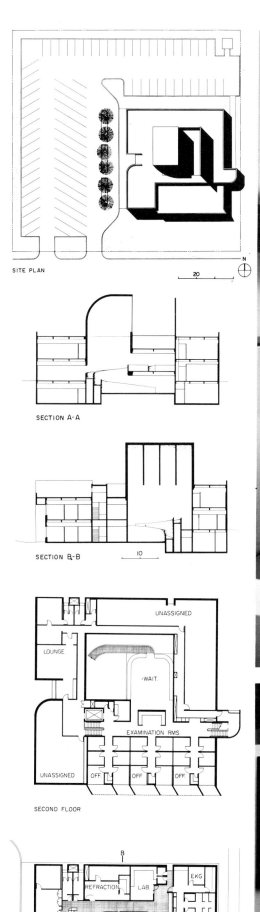

SITE PLAN

20 N

SECTION A-A

SECTION B-B

10

UNASSIGNED

LOUNGE

WAIT

EXAMINATION RMS.

UNASSIGNED OFF. OFF. OFF.

SECOND FLOOR

REFRACTION LAB. E.K.G.

RECEPT. X-RAY

A A

WAIT

UP DN X-RAY

INJECT. EXAMINATION ROOMS

PHARM. OFF. OFF. OFF.

FIRST FLOOR B 10 N

A jubilant remodelling of this Manhattan structure laminates a community's present to its remembered past

Van Brody photos

At least one building among the deteriorating tenement facades of West 54th Street in Manhattan is bright and inviting—as city life and its institutions can be. It is the Clinton Youth and Family Center, once the Seventh District Police Court building. The painted metal doors, windows and new intake pipes for air conditioning make vigorous images for the future, and have at the same time been fitted within the orderly stonework of the past; they seem to say that we need not insist on historically accurate restorations to provide a necessary feeling of continuity with our roots, nor do we need to level old architecture to make cities better. The Youth and Family Center is operated by the YMCA of Greater New York and the Rotary Club of New York, and the majority of the renovation costs were paid for by the Astor Foundation, which has funded several other building projects of notable worth in New York's ghetto neighborhoods. James Stewart Polshek, along with Walfredo Toscanini, were the architects. A fine, old building has been "added" to New York, and similar buildings, sound of body but needing a fresh new spirit, could be added in many of our cities.

Inside, the old six-story structure built at the beginning of this century has been transformed by brightly painted walls, movable/storable furniture, and plenty of irreverent writing on the walls. The surprisingly appropriate flowing spaces house noisy children and under-financed neighborhood health programs as well as they once housed the solemn, not-too-happy processes of criminal justice. By removing several full-height brick walls erected during previous remodelings, the vaulted solemnity of the old main entrance lobby (top, right) was reclaimed. But elsewhere on the ground floor, in the new lounge and the entrance foyer to the elevators (right and following page), color rather than space has been added. The old wall planes, moldings and right angles have been properly violated by paint in diagonal stripes and overlapping circles, yet the sense of old architecture conserved still remains. This large ground floor space is a kind of "mixing valve" where all of the diverse groups coming in and out of the center each day are brought together.

The center can be understood as having its large-group "mixer" spaces—including the gymnasium—on the lower floors, the park in back, and the progressively smaller and more private-use spaces on the upper floors. The central staircase that connects them all is a finely scaled circular shaft (see isometric, following page) filled with open wrought iron lattice work and skylighted at the top. The center of the shaft used to be occupied by an elevator—the only one in the original court—that unfortunately had to be removed. The old main courtroom is now the gymnasium, with a new maple floor and with bouncing balls and the arc of their travel painted boldly on the brick walls. The coffered ceiling of the courtroom provided excellent recesses for new lighting fixtures, and a classical portico that was a feature of the courtroom has been allowed to remain, now framing a basketball backboard. A second, low-ceilinged courtroom occupied what is now the fourth and fifth floors, but there was no need for a second large space. So, it has been divided into seminar rooms and offices (see isometric, p. 26) and most of the new partitions on this floor are surfaced with hardboard and left unpainted. These fourth and fifth floors have wall-to-wall carpeting throughout, and they are—not surprisingly—among the most popular for smaller meetings and games.

The renovation commission was received by the architects in 1968, and the project was complete in 1970; it took one year to prepare contract documents and about 18 months for construction. The original contract called for about $400,000 in work, but the cost of the project rose to almost $1 million through change-order additions during construction, as the fund-raising drives became more successful and additional money became available for additional work.

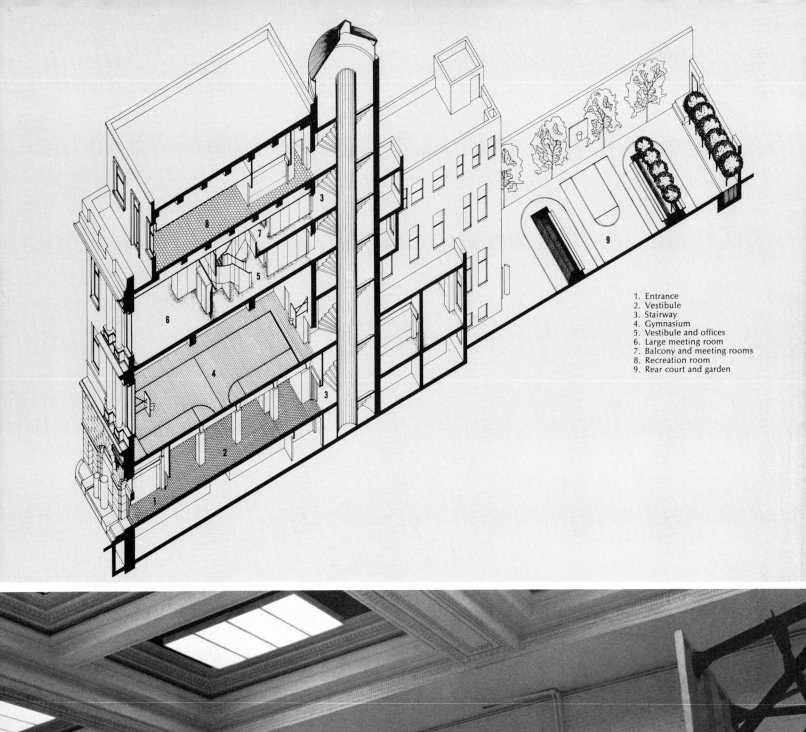

1. Entrance
2. Vestibule
3. Stairway
4. Gymnasium
5. Vestibule and offices
6. Large meeting room
7. Balcony and meeting rooms
8. Recreation room
9. Rear court and garden

The large meeting room on the fourth floor (below) exhibits the graphic skill and color that makes the center as a whole so successful. The three dimensionality of the windows is painted on, not real, but it is almost better this way. The stair to the fifth floor mezzanine (below) shows how the unpainted hardboard is used in conjunction with the red carpet, to achieve a remarkable feeling of richness with inexpensive, wear-resistant surfaces. The rear garden (photo right) was once the site of one of the most decrepit jails in Manhattan, torn down in the course of this remodeling at a cost of $90,000. Now the trees are beginning to grow there, to complement the painted trees on the walls.

CLINTON YOUTH AND FAMILY CENTER, New York City. Architects: *James Stewart Polshek and Associates, and Walfredo Toscanini—J.S. Polshek*, project architect. Graphic design: *James Stewart Polshek and Associates—David Bliss*, project designer. Mechanical and electrical engineers: *Benjamin & Zicherman Associates*; general contractor: *Dember Construction Corp.*

Stan Menscher photo

INTERIORS FOR TEACHING

In education, the most widely discussed and visible changes have appeared in the design of elementary schools. The open plan, in all its shadings and variations, has found wider acceptance among teachers, parents and youngsters. Often tentative, sometimes grudging, this acceptance has not been complete and most open plan installations make provision for the erection of standard classroom partitions should experiments in open planning prove generally unsuccessful.

Three elementary schools are included in this section. Each shows a different modification to the concept of absolute openness. In Paul Rudolph's design for Chorley Elementary School (page 30) in Middletown, New York, changes of level and half height partitions help create important spatial definitions. The Kent Elementary School, in Boston, by Earl R. Flansburgh & Associates, utilizes two fixed and two folding partitions so that the degree of closure can be adjusted to suit the circumstance. At Parma, Ohio, Don Hisaka's Crile Elementary School is a traditional plan modified by skillful design to provide a large open media center. The reader will see for himself that acoustical control was essential in all these designs and that the architects went to some pains to secure it.

Much was heard during these years about windowless schools although few were built. Even in big city ghettos, where vandalism and unfocused hostility make windows·especially vulnerable, few school systems have been willing to authorize designs that completely sealed the classrooms to natural light. Lighting levels, particularly over work and study areas, have been raised, but this vector will almost certainly be blunted by a national energy crisis.

At post secondary and college levels, new attitudes and new technology have created new forms like computer centers or the Communications Building (page 51) by Perkins & Will for the State University of New York. Existing forms have also been reshaped. The renaissance of the community college and the reinvestment in vocational education (now called career education) in the late '60s began to seriously challenge the designers of new educational facilities. And the press of continuing education will make demands on designer's skill at least as great as any they have heretofore had to face.

Joseph W. Molitor photos

Vigorous expression of structure and flexible teaching spaces for a suburban school

The program given architect Paul Rudolph for the John W. Chorley Elementary School required spaces adaptable not just to team teaching, but to a "continuous progress plan" that abolishes grade levels and separates children only by age. Within these groups, each child moves almost independently towards standards in each subject established by his own potential.

Rudolph's design reflects this program

precisely. Three wings or houses (for age groups paralleling grades K-2, 3 and 4, and 5 and 6) step up or down the sloping site from a strong central spine. Other main blocks, shown in the perspective, are the gymnasium complex (foreground) and a fourth wing (right rear) for educable and trainable children. The stepped design relates not just to the program and the site, but to the teaching methods used and the

simple and low-cost construction system.

Inside and out, the school demonstrates the sense of surprise, the seeming complexity but essential simplicity, and the three-dimensionality that mark so much of Rudolph's work.

Inside each of the houses the space can be opened wide, or subdivided as needed, by accordion partitions. Even the broad traffic areas between pairs of rooms are used during classroom periods as spaces where children can retreat from the general classroom activity. With the partitions thrown back, the stepped-down spaces offer excellent sight-lines, functioning much as a conventional auditorium does for group instruction. The carpeting, the porous ceiling material, and the "steps" of both floor and ceiling keep noise and clatter to an acceptable level.

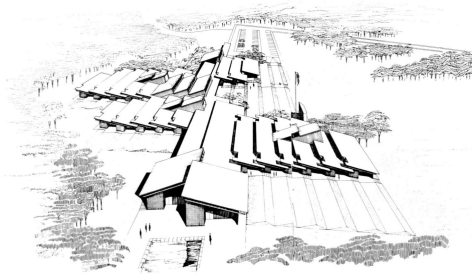

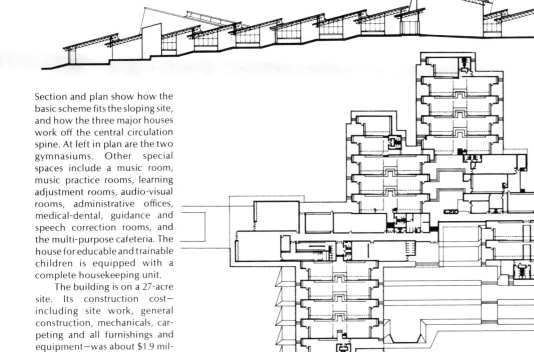

Section and plan show how the basic scheme fits the sloping site, and how the three major houses work off the central circulation spine. At left in plan are the two gymnasiums. Other special spaces include a music room, music practice rooms, learning adjustment rooms, audio-visual rooms, administrative offices, medical-dental, guidance and speech correction rooms, and the multi-purpose cafeteria. The house for educable and trainable children is equipped with a complete housekeeping unit.

The building is on a 27-acre site. Its construction cost—including site work, general construction, mechanicals, carpeting and all furnishings and equipment—was about $1.9 million.

Color, in the felt pennants, kites and mobiles hung from the ceiling, in children's art on windows (see below), in plants and in other kinds of small spots everywhere, gives "a sense of joyfulness" to what is essentially very plainly finished space. The steelwork, the roof deck, the service lines, and the block walls are frankly exposed and handled in neutral greys and white. The photo (p. 32) shows the main open space—used not just as cafeteria, but as auditorium, music and lecture room, and for PTA meetings. The trafficway is typical of the "step-up" arrangement throughout the building. Photo (p. 32) shows the wall at the lowest level of the big space, complete with one of the school's continuously changing and colorful art exhibits.

The library is centrally located just off the main circulation spine and convenient to all three houses. It is partitioned from the corridor by a low wall with glass above, so that light from beyond the corridor can flood in. The space is readily changed into classroom space should program requirements change. The photos below show one of the several supervisory alcoves perched above the classroom spaces and reached by a stair off the traffic area. Each teacher within the house has a work space for lesson preparation. These monitor spaces are lighted by large glass areas that spill light onto the traffic areas below.

An innovative and functional interpretation of a traditional teaching program

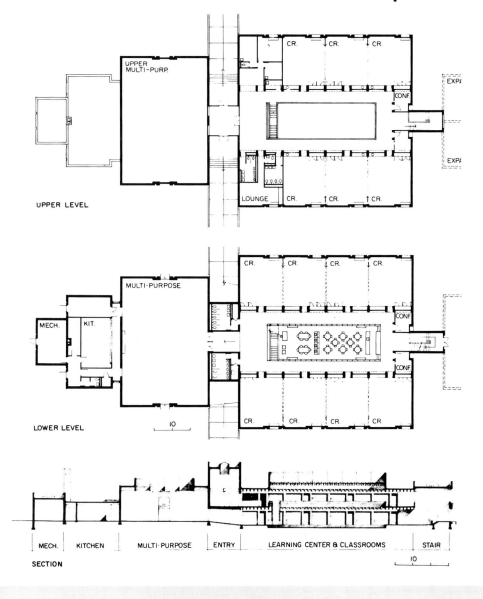

UPPER LEVEL

LOWER LEVEL

MECH.   KITCHEN   MULTI-PURPOSE   ENTRY   LEARNING CENTER & CLASSROOMS   STAIR

SECTION

This elementary school for a Cleveland suburb by Don M. Hisaka and Associates is a persuasive example of what can be accomplished when architectural inventiveness is brought to bear on a traditional school program. Growing out of a program that called for a single-story, 14-classroom school with an orthodox library, the plan that finally evolved is far from conventional. Through a continuous dialogue with the client and with the sympathetic help of school superintendent Dr. Stuart Openlander, Hisaka was permitted to expand the library into a double height resource center flanked by two levels of classrooms. Lower level classrooms are assigned to older children whose use of the resource center is more continual. The main entrance is ramped (see photo left) so that entry is at the upper level near the administrative and staff spaces. A multi-purpose room, kitchen, mechanical space and shop complete the plan.

Imaginative planning, coupled with thoughtful attention to detail, brought this school in under budget—and contributed to its receiving a First Honor Award from the Ohio Chapter of the American Institute of Architects.

CRILE ELEMENTARY SCHOOL, Parma, Ohio. Architects: *Don M. Hisaka and Associates (Robert Barclay, project manager)* structural engineers: *R. M. Gensert & Associates;* mechanical engineers: *George Evans & Associates;* electrical engineers: *William Ferguson & Associates.*

Thom Abel photos

Resource center (above) is both physically and symbolically the school's nucleus. Conceived as a one-room schoolhouse, this exceptionally handsome space is defined by classrooms and day-lighted by a clerestory above. Balcony and roof soffits are formed by cantilevered double tees supported on masonry piers.

Materials are simple: load-bearing masonry for walls and piers, concrete block, trimmed with wood, for parapets and stair. Detailing throughout is simple and appealing. Rich brown carpeting contrasts warmly with buff-colored masonry. Color accents are provided freely by books, artwork and the children.

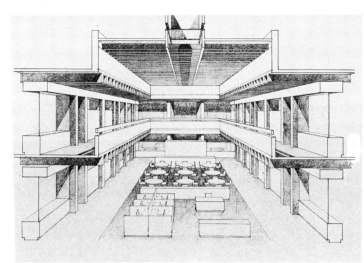

Alexandre Georges photos

Special teaching spaces designed to meet the needs of Jacksonville's exceptional children

Because mental retardation occurs with predictable frequency and cuts impartially across all racial and socio-economic lines, every large community can predict with surprising accuracy the incidence of retardation it can expect among its young. Jacksonville's school authorities, intent on helping such unlucky youngsters, commissioned a separate facility for 150 children to replace the special classes they had previously attended at various dispersed locations. Utilizing a heavily wooded site, set well back from the road, William Morgan developed a plan that pivots four classroom clusters around a central assembly area. Most of the children suffer from hypertension. They are easily excited by unexpected sights or sounds. And because such hypertension is infectious, each classroom is fitted with a small "time-out" room (see plan) where an excited youngster can be isolated until he regains his composure. Other special adaptations include a therapy pool centered in the administration spaces and the deliberate installation of a wide variety of door and window hardware. The advanced pavilion includes a family living area and model apartment where girls learn domestic skills and a shop where older boys receive pre-occupational training.

SCHOOL FOR EXCEPTIONAL CHILDREN, Jacksonville, Florida. Architect: *William Morgan;* structural engineer: *H. W. Keister;* mechanical and electrical engineers: *Evans & Hammond, Inc.;* contractor: *Newman Construction Company.*

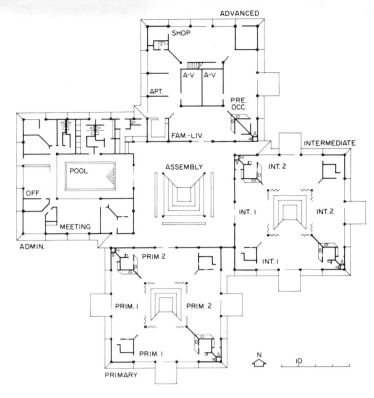

The classroom clusters, each with its pyramid roof, give the plan its visual order and reflect the school's domestic, non-institutional character. The central assembly area (photo below) doubles as a cafeteria and is used in the evening for adult education. The structure is concrete frame, exterior walls are light brown brick, ceilings and soffits are heavy pine plank. Orange carpeting, set against a generally neutral background gives these spaces an uncommon warmth and unity.

William Kent Elementary School, Boston: complex space simply detailed

Entry and vertical circulation are contained in a dramatically sky-lighted, four-story volume. The exterior brick is carried inside for continuity and the stair landings, framed out using exposed steel, are fitted with double height pipe-railings for the protection of youngsters. The same pipe-railing is used for handrail, but augmented by a lower wood rail for the use of smaller children.

Flansburgh originally conceived the space as part of a public circulation route through the community. These plans were later dropped at the request of the school board, but the tall space with its vigorous expression of level retains much of the strength of its first conception. In spite of its apparent height, the viewer is not "shrunk." The eye is drawn rhythmically upward, pausing a moment at each level, and easily finding release through a canted skylight over the entrance to the teachers' fifth floor lounge. For a school, it is a surprisingly powerful spatial composition. But for so steeply contoured a site, it seems especially appropriate to express the elements of vertical circulation with force and conviction.

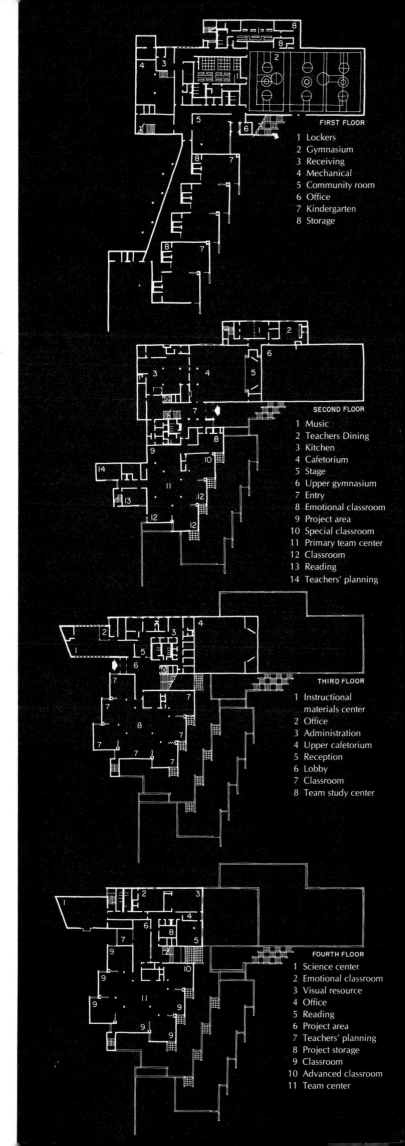

FIRST FLOOR

1 Lockers
2 Gymnasium
3 Receiving
4 Mechanical
5 Community room
6 Office
7 Kindergarten
8 Storage

SECOND FLOOR

1 Music
2 Teachers Dining
3 Kitchen
4 Cafetorium
5 Stage
6 Upper gymnasium
7 Entry
8 Emotional classroom
9 Project area
10 Special classroom
11 Primary team center
12 Classroom
13 Reading
14 Teachers' planning

THIRD FLOOR

1 Instructional
   materials center
2 Office
3 Administration
4 Upper cafetorium
5 Reception
6 Lobby
7 Classroom
8 Team study center

FOURTH FLOOR

1 Science center
2 Emotional classroom
3 Visual resource
4 Office
5 Reading
6 Project area
7 Teachers' planning
8 Project storage
9 Classroom
10 Advanced classroom
11 Team center

Classrooms, according to local code, require a full sprinkler system if they extend upward beyond four floors. For this reason, the fifth floor at the William Kent School is reserved for teachers' lounges and services. Each regular classroom space—most are for unstructured classes—has two fixed walls and either one or two operable, three-quarter height partitions that provide visual enclosure but not acoustical privacy. All the classroom spaces are carpeted and hung ceilings are finished in acoustical tile. Lighting fixtures have been boxed out to effectively lower the ceiling height and modulate the larger spaces (photo above). A supergraphic series of numerals identify the teaching spaces and add color enrichment (photo right). The same concern for simple and appealing detail exists throughout the classroom and kindergarten areas to give the Kent Elementary School a welcome design unity.

WILLIAM KENT ELEMENTARY SCHOOL, Boston, Massachusetts. Owner: *City of Boston.* Architects: *Earl R. Flansburgh and Associates, Inc.*—design team: *Earl R. Flansburgh, Russell F. Tremaine associate;* interior furnishings: *Linda Stuart associate.* Engineers: *Alonzo B. Reed Co., Inc.* Landscape architects: *Mason & Frey.* General contractor: *E. C. Blanchard, Inc.*

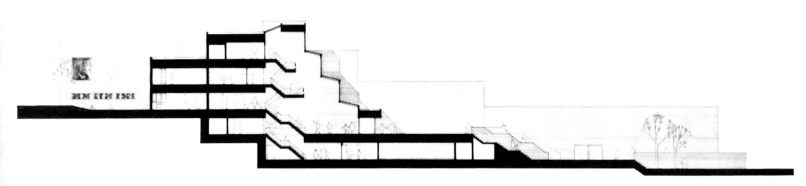

Ezra Stoller © ESTO

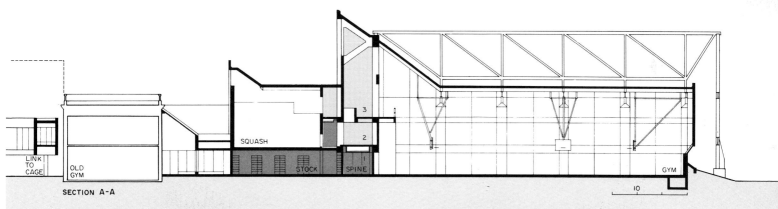

SECTION A-A

LINK TO CAGE OLD GYM SQUASH STOCK SPINE GYM 10

A muscular new structure at Exeter for teaching and developing athletic skills

This 216,000 square-foot athletic facility is highly legible as a design despite its great size and its multi-scaled elements which fit together with the intricacy of a Chinese puzzle. As the section (above) indicates, the new building is attached to the older gym by a low element containing the mud room and trainer space. The squash court shown above the first (or basement) level is one of twelve—three in the entrance wing shown in the photos (left and below), seven in the long wing through which this section has been taken, and two for exhibition purposes where the two wings intersect at the corner (see plans, page 44).

In section the squash courts are like small chapels—their front walls washed with light from hidden skylights, their rear walls opening upon a teaching gallery. Below the gallery is a narrow corridor which is part of the circulation network for athletes—one of three principal halls, the top two of which are the main axes of the visitor circulation network. All three, taken together form the building's spine.

The spine with its continuous skylight dominates the building from within and without. Its roof is dramatically framed with precast concrete struts, formed on the site, which act as counterforces to the steel trusses which support roofs of gym, pool and rinks.

The high ramped entrance faces the campus and is used by students and faculty, while the other (opposite page) faces the town and is used by the public.

New gymnasia are almost always expressed as volumes. At Exeter the architects have expressed a structural system and a forceful circulation network, rather than a volume or series of volumes. This approach, which recognized the fact that the building would be huge, has produced a new and highly appropriate urbanistic scale for the new facility, within a system which permits continuous expansion. To express this infinite expansibility, the architects wished a truss to appear at each modular point even where end walls, which are likely to be permanent, could be made bearing. They were also aware

that the only trusses to be completely legible to the viewer on the ground would be those located at the end walls of each wing. Since the trusses cost between $40 and $50 thousand each, however, legibility and the expression of expansibility lost priority. As the roof plan now shows, only one truss appears where a bearing wall would do. It is not certain that the wing will expand in this direction, but the principle of legibility has been upheld, particularly since this truss is adjacent to the main entrance and can be seen by everyone.

The diagram (p. 44) indicates the complexity of circulation patterns required to serve a variety of athletic functions. The photos (p. 45) were made within the portion of the building which turns the corner and acts as the link between the two wings. Visitor space (see photos) displays student art and overlooks the exercise room (see plan). The exterior photo (above) was made at the intersection of the two wings at the hub or linking element.

The spine of the Exeter physical education building, like an attenua-

ted cathedral nave, thrusts its way past the swimming pool, squash courts, and huge gymnasium to come to rest between two hockey rinks (plan). Like flying buttresses, the precast concrete struts resist forces generated by the roof trusses coming to rest on concrete girders supported by paired columns on opposite sides of the spine.

The exterior truss system provides a visually clean interior which reduces distraction for everyone following the ball or watching a dive, as the photos indicate.

The swimming pool is 60 feet wide by 75 feet long, with eight racing lanes. It has large deck areas for teaching and exercising. Seating for 450 has been provided in permanent bleachers. Moveable bleachers will seat another 200 spectators.

The gymnasium has a total floor dimension of 115 by 200 feet. Its size permits the simultaneous use for basketball of three cross courts (50 feet by 84 feet) separated by two divider curtains. Alternatively it also permits the simultaneous use of one main court, 50 feet by 94 feet, with

43

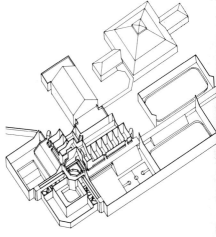

SECOND LEVEL

THIRD LEVEL

FIRST LEVEL

ROOF PLAN

CAGE RUNNING TRACK

CAGE

CAGE

CAGE

HOCKEY

HOCKEY

HOCKEY

SQUASH

SQUASH

OLD GYM

SQUASH

GYM

EXERCISE

GALLERY

OFF

OFF

POOL

BLEACHERS

GYM

EXERCISE

POOL

HOCKEY

GYM

LOCKERS

FACULTY

EXERCISE

SHOWERS

LOCKERS

POOL

A

A

HOCKEY

HOCKEY

NEW LINK

OLD GYM

GYM

POOL

20

ATHLETES

eighteen rows of folding bleacher seating for a total of 900 spectators; plus one cross court 50 feet by 84 feet separated by a divider curtain from the main court.

The two ice hockey rinks are each 85 feet by 185 feet. The rink in which the public matches are played seats 600.

The building has ten regular squash courts with a teaching gallery running through all courts and two exhibition courts with seating for 100 spectators each.

All sports areas have openings arranged to avoid direct sunlight, as can be seen in all the photos on this page. Office spaces are also lit by indirect natural light.

Early in the design of the Exeter gym, structural engineer William LeMessurier began to collaborate with the architects in the development of an appropriate structural system. All were agreed that they did not want a dramatic structural shape to dominate the interior spaces, and that interior trusses, in particular, were distracting to players and spectators alike. The maximum spans of 130 feet were great enough to constitute an interesting design problem, but not so wide as to call for anything so spectacular as an arch.

Deep trusses cost less than shallow trusses, but if they are located inside the structure this saving is offset by the cost of the enclosing materials. It was decided, therefore, that the trusses would be located outside the roof.

Because conventional single-plane trusses would have needed subsidiary cross bracing, LeMessurier designed a three-dimensional truss which, as such, is self-cross bracing. Because of its own inner rigidity and ability to resist lateral wind loads each truss was shipped whole from a plant in Portland, Maine. Most trusses shipped this way require a flat-bed truck. The LeMessurier truss simply required wheels at one end and a tractor at the other. Only 10 feet wide by 15 feet deep, the trusses had no difficulty passing under bridges en route.

The trusses are designed with

rigidity and ability to resist lateral wind loads each truss was shipped whole from a plant in Portland, Maine. Most trusses shipped this way require a flat-bed truck. The LeMessurier truss simply required wheels at one end and a tractor at the other. Only 10 feet wide by 15 feet deep, the trusses had no difficulty passing under bridges en route.

The trusses are designed with two parallel compression members at the top and one member in tension at the bottom. For strict economy, the trusses should have been reversed with two compression members at the bottom and a single tension member at the top. The supporting legs would have been shorter and the interior spans, supported on pairs of points would have been shorter and lighter. There is no question, however, that the appearance of the trusses as finally executed justifies their design.

The Exeter gym has the first architect-designed structural frame to be built out of weathering steel pipe. The vertical supports, also made of weathering steel, are set off from the body of the building like insect legs so that drips from the rusting structure will not stain the concrete wall panels. These supports, of course, could have been concealed within the wall more cheaply, but their powerful, almost athletic stance appears to validate the extra cost.

The Exeter gym has a total of 15 weathering steel trusses. Eleven are 130 feet long and weigh 22 tons each. These cover the sports halls with spectator seating. Four trusses are 110 feet long and weigh 18 tons each. They span the hockey rink without spectator seating, and can be seen at their point of contact with the roof in the photo (above). At the points along the central spine in which the large sports halls with their long spans lie opposite the squash courts with their short spans, the precast concrete struts (right), no longer parallel, form a series of V's. The bridge (below) connects the new gym with an existing indoor track. Cost of the new complex was $5.375 million or $26.5 per square foot.

NEW ATHLETICS FACILITY, Exeter, New Hampshire. Owner: *The Phillips Exeter Academy.* Architects: *Kallmann & McKinnell*—project manager: *Jeffrey Brown;* job captain: *Donnelly Erdman;* structural engineers: *LeMessurier Associates*—associate-in-charge: *Hans William Hagen;* mechanical engineers: *Francis Associates;* acoustical consultants: *Bolt Beranek & Newman;* cost consultant: *Industrial Estimating Service;* general contractor: *George B. H. Macomber Company.*

A Canadian college for the applied arts that stimulates enormous visual excitement

Sheridan College is a complex of one- and two-story steel structures growing in stages on a handsome site outside Toronto. The site was formerly farmland and is bisected by a shallow stream. The buildings, both existing and proposed, will be grouped around the stream and will grow outward in a finger pattern as later stages are built.

The college, of course, provides a variety of spaces, but the basic structure, which had to be assembled on a tight schedule, is a 30 by 30-foot bay with built up roofing over a steel roof deck. Triangular trusses support the roof deck and a pair of long Vierendeel girders carry the trusses (see photos). The bays are arranged on each side of an elevated spine from which overviews of skylighted studios are provided on each side. All services have been left exposed for maximum flexibility. Ductwork, structural hardware and conduit, therefore, become integral parts of the interior design. It is gratifying to see them assembled so convincingly into a coherent, evocative and colorful visual whole.

SHERIDAN COLLEGE, Oakville, Ontario. Architects: *Marani, Rounthwaite & Dick—Klaus Donker, designer; Keith Wagland, planner; David Freeman, project manager; A. Cosway, cost control; C. F. T. Rounthwaite, partner-in-charge;* engineers: *Kleinfelt & Associates* (structural); *Rybka Smith & Ginsler* (mechanical/electrical); landscape architect: *Don Hancock;* contractor: *Mitchell Construction.*

George Zimbel photos

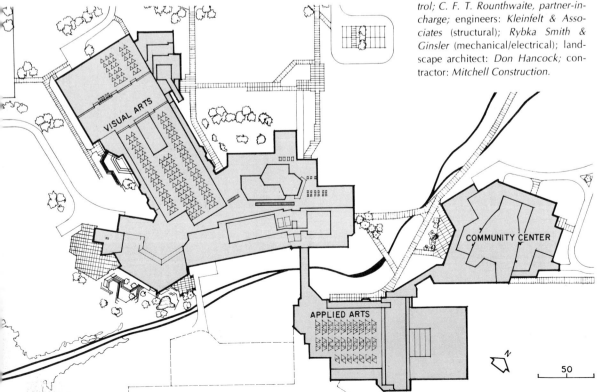

Sheridan students gather for coffee and talk (top photo) in a small cluster defined by low partitions and floated in the enlarged corridor. Demountable, bleacher seating is provided in the large-scale work spaces (center photo). These large studio spaces are lighted by a combination of fluorescent tubing and natural daylight admitted through a regular pattern of pyramidal skylights. Faculty desks (photo below) overlook the studios in both directions from the elevated gallery. These spaces, large and small, are filled with exciting color and activity.

Bethlehem Steel Corporation

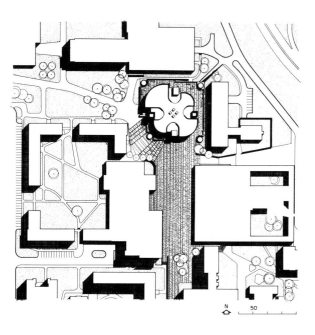

A communications center where the teachers learn as much as the students

The second floor—actually fourth level above grade—groups instructional areas of various types around the central student lounge (see page 53). Two of the three tiered halls seat 50, one seats 185 students. The fourth space has a level floor and is divided into four 50-seat rooms now being used as a media-methods-materials complex. Preparation rooms have been converted to self-instruction labs in audio-visual equipment use, a change from the original intent.

Both mezzanine floors are restricted areas for use by staff and technicians who load rear-screen projectors for presentation in lecture halls below. Plan at right shows how mezzanine works with circulation system to handle student traffic circulation expeditiously: lecture hall entrance is at lower level of tiered hall, exit is at upper level. Stairs are at side of each hall, connecting directly with entrances to building at grade level. Preparation rooms next to each hall were originally intended for use by faculty in setting up demonstrations and exhibits, but sophistication of building and equipment requires earlier and more intricate planning, now done in "nerve center" in basement. Prep rooms are used now on assignment for design and planning of courses.

Oval shape of building is broken at four points for entrances and stair towers (which serve as bearing walls). Below grade is "nerve center" for campus communication by television and audio signal. Here also are library, resource center, workshops and consultation rooms.

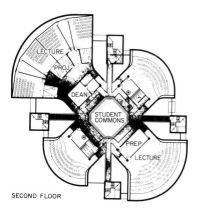

SECOND FLOOR

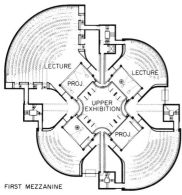

FIRST MEZZANINE

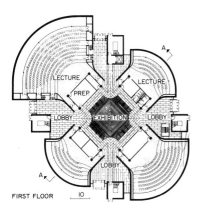

FIRST FLOOR

The new Communications Center at the State University of New York at Buffalo is a highly sophisticated instrument for the preparation, distribution and use of multi-media instructional materials. Within its curving walls are concentrated communications facilities that serve all departments of the campus. For development of courses to be given effectively to groups of students ranging in number from 50 to 400, there are facilities for programing extensive use of films, slides, tapes and other audio-visual materials, and consultants with whom to discuss such programing. For televising (live or taped) programs to lecture halls in the building or to classrooms elsewhere on campus, there are three professionally-equipped television studios. For instruction, there are 11 lecture halls of various sizes and types, some tiered, some level-floored, currently serving some 1300 students per day. Although the plans suggest a building of high specificity, the spaces originally intended for one use have been adapted to other uses without disruption either to themselves or to the rest of the building. The flexibility of the lobby and of the student lounge areas also make the building usable for an even broader program of communications. Because the multi-media approach to instruction is a relatively new field, and because the need for effective means of handling large numbers of students is increasingly important, one of the 185-seat halls has been equipped as an experiment in student response to presentations. Among questions to which answers are sought are these: how many visuals can be assimilated at one time? How long should each visual be displayed for maximum retention of information? How large should a visual be for effective impact? Does placement on the screen affect the learning process? The Communications Center was built at a cost of $2,157,000, or $27.09 per square foot.

LECTURE HALL CENTER, STATE UNIVERSITY OF NEW YORK, Buffalo, New York. Architects: *The Perkins & Will Partnership—Wesley V. Pipher, partner-in-charge; Richard Maitland, designer;* mechanical consultants: *Syska & Hennesey;* structural consultants: *Garfinkel & Marenberg;* general contractor: *John W. Cowper Co.*

Louis Reens photos

Dramatic two-story entrance lobby serves also as down-lighted exhibit area or, partitioned, can become from one to four seminar rooms. Concrete bridges at mezzanine connect rear-projection equipment rooms. Clinker brick, used for exterior, is carried inside to lobby.

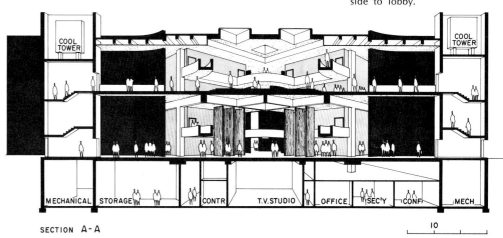

SECTION A-A   10

Louis Reens photos

Large lecture halls seat up to 400; are equipped for rear and overhead projection with all controls at instructor's lectern in front. Screens are 30-feet wide, 10-feet high. Ceiling spots highlight special exhibits. Student lounge (right) is raised platform in center of top floor. Platform has also been successfully used as arena theater.

William Doran photo

Gund Hall unites the design disciplines under a single powerful trussed roof form

The central studio at Gund Hall brings together for the first time in fifty years all programs within the Graduate School of Design at Harvard. It brings them together physically and as a symbol of the GSD, but it will take time to learn whether these separate entities—Department of Architecture, City and Regional Planning, Landscape Architecture, The Urban Design Program, The Program for Advanced Environmental Studies, and the Laboratory for Computer Graphics and Spacial Analysis—can work together as an interdisciplinary unit, without hierarchy, as intended. As the section shows, there are areas at the back of each level where individuals or groups may have securely private spaces if they choose.

The studio is clearly a success as the symbol it wanted to be. Once committed to undifferentiated space, it would have been wrong to put in columns or walls to save money, and the architects were able to resist these pressures from sources within Harvard. One has difficulty relating the studio to known spaces; there are feelings of a stadium about it, or an indoor track or some qualities of a cathedral. The ambient noise from the air conditioning is high, which helps eliminate sharp noises from the general clatter of a drafting room. The space is surprisingly quiet; you can hold a conversation at normal levels and your words are not overheard across the room. From the way the students have arranged themselves

in the first four weeks, the drafting boards out in the open are apparently more desirable than those under the low ceilings, and the boards right at the edge of the "cliffs" seem the hottest property of all.

GUND HALL GRADUATE SCHOOL OF DESIGN, Harvard University, Cambridge, Massachusetts, Architect: *John Andrews, Architects—John Andrews, Edward R. Baldwin and John Simpson,* designers; *Edward R. Baldwin,* partner-in-charge. Engineers: *LeMessurier Associates* (structural); *G. Granek & Associates* (mechanical); *Jack Chisvin & Assoc.* (electrical). Cost consultants: *Helyar, Vermeulen, Rae & Mauchan.* Landscape architects: *Richard Strong Associates.* Specifications: *Wood, Angus & Owen Inc.* Acoustical: *Harold R. Mull & Assoc.* Contractor: *J. Slotnik Co.*

Len Gittleman

1 Audio visual
2 Circulation
3 Library
4 Technology workshop
5 Exhibition
6 Design workshop
7 Studios
8 Faculty offices
9 Microforms and maps
10 Mechanical tunnel

SECTION

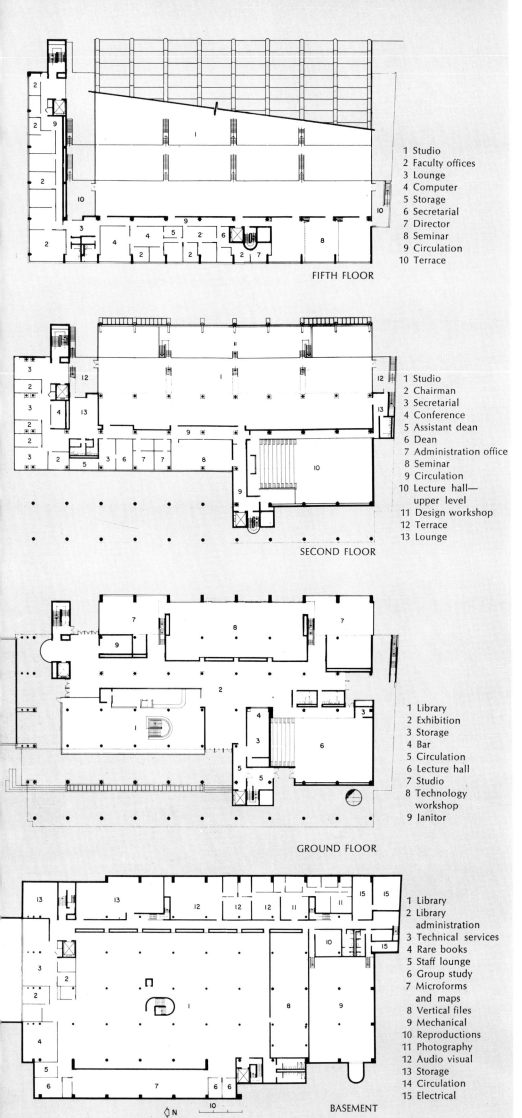

FIFTH FLOOR

1 Studio
2 Faculty offices
3 Lounge
4 Computer
5 Storage
6 Secretarial
7 Director
8 Seminar
9 Circulation
10 Terrace

SECOND FLOOR

1 Studio
2 Chairman
3 Secretarial
4 Conference
5 Assistant dean
6 Dean
7 Administration office
8 Seminar
9 Circulation
10 Lecture hall—
   upper level
11 Design workshop
12 Terrace
13 Lounge

GROUND FLOOR

1 Library
2 Exhibition
3 Storage
4 Bar
5 Circulation
6 Lecture hall
7 Studio
8 Technology
   workshop
9 Janitor

BASEMENT

1 Library
2 Library
   administration
3 Technical services
4 Rare books
5 Staff lounge
6 Group study
7 Microforms
   and maps
8 Vertical files
9 Mechanical
10 Reproductions
11 Photography
12 Audio visual
13 Storage
14 Circulation
15 Electrical

◇ N

Loeb Library and the auditorium occupy most of the ground floor, with the largest portion of the library space in the basement. Loeb Library houses 155,000 volumes and has become a major architectural collection. The building may be expanded if necessary from the point of the stair tower at the end of the shorter office wing, shown in the plans at left. Gund Hall now contains over 150,000 square feet of floor space, with space for 500 students, about 80 faculty, and 50 administration including library and workshop staffs. The building is air-conditioned using chilled water from the Harvard central utility plant, and it is heated through high-pressure steam from the same source.

Steve Rosenthal photos

This first building for the University of Lethbridge has a superb location overlooking the valley of the Oldman River and the city of Lethbridge. It fits into the undulations of its site, using the contours to its advantage and for its own purposes, so that its height varies while its roof line remains constant, a flat plane that hardly rises above the line of the horizon.

Within this one building are contained all the parts that make up a university: student residences, classrooms, laboratories, offices for administration, faculty and student activities, library, bookstore, dining room, snack bar—everything except Fine Arts and Physical Education which have their own building (Project 1A, Robins Mitchell Watson, architects). So complete an integration of residential and learning spaces in one structure is rare if not unique, but here it represents an architectural response to the academic goals set up in 1967 by the University Planning Committee which include "flexibility and openness to innovation; encouragement to the highest degree of interaction between students and faculty; fostering the spirit of free inquiry and the critical interpretation of ideas." The essential character of the University was that it was to be a place where, as its first president, Sam Smith, said, "everything can happen at once" and where there would be "a chance to make the whole person," and much of this intent has been realized. But not all of it, and not exactly in the way it was first envisioned. The ideal toward which everyone —Planning Committee and architects—worked was splendid but, in the end and in very human terms, unrealistic. It was an ideal embodied in accounts of El Azhar, the 9th century center of Islamic teaching, a sort of "educational marketplace" where students, merchants, scholars and beggars gathered, mostly

Megastructure for learning and living on Western Canada's empty prairie landscape

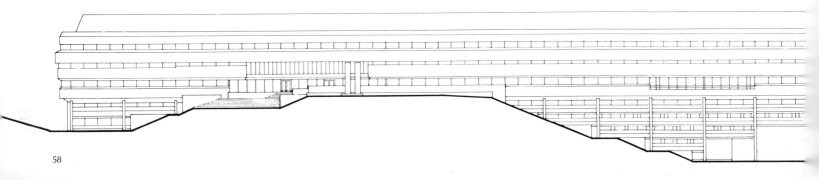

"A distillation of all the elements into earth and sky," is Arthur Erickson's description of the prairie landscape at the edge of which the new University is situated. "Objects caught between earth and sky appear trivial unless they emerge intrinsically from one or the other or unless they reflect in generosity of size the prairie scale."

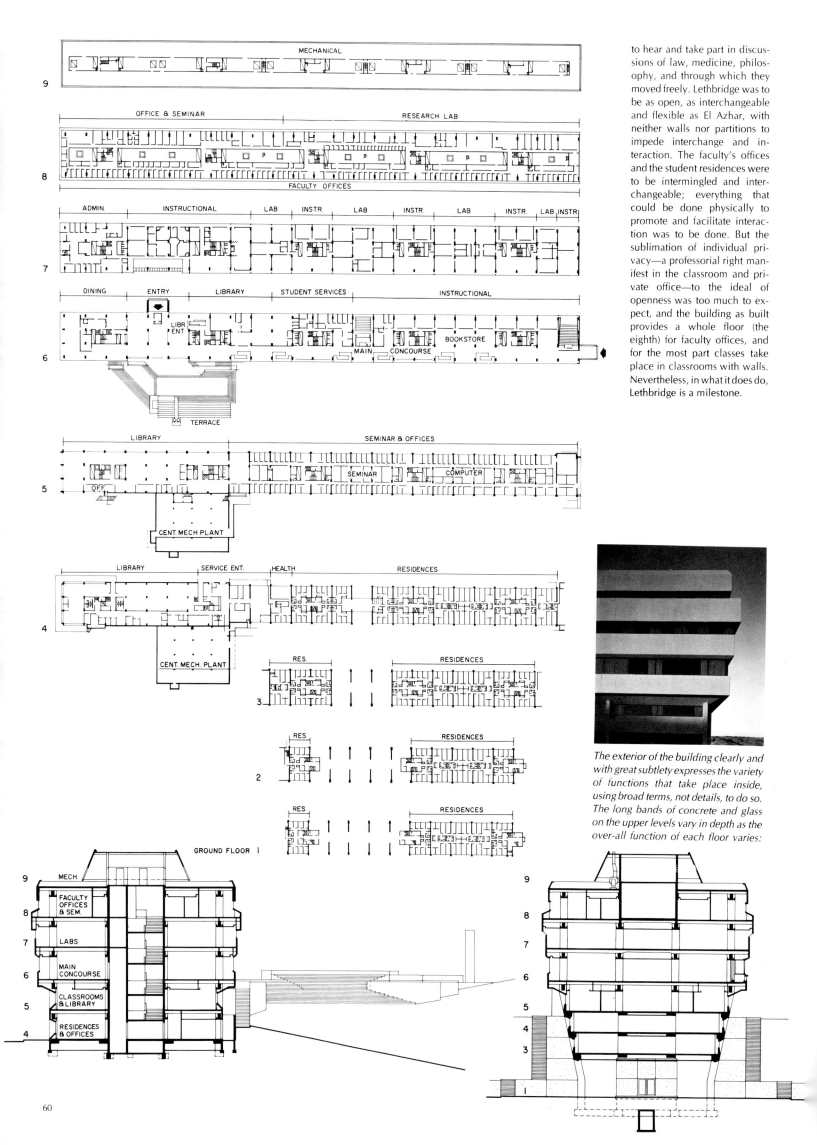

9 MECHANICAL

8 OFFICE & SEMINAR — RESEARCH LAB / FACULTY OFFICES

7 ADMIN. INSTRUCTIONAL LAB INSTR. LAB INSTR. LAB INSTR. LAB INSTR

6 DINING ENTRY LIBRARY STUDENT SERVICES INSTRUCTIONAL / LIBR. ENT. / MAIN CONCOURSE / BOOKSTORE / TERRACE

5 LIBRARY SEMINAR & OFFICES / OFF. / SEMINAR COMPUTER / CENT. MECH PLANT

4 LIBRARY SERVICE ENT. HEALTH RESIDENCES / CENT. MECH. PLANT

3 RES. RESIDENCES

2 RES. RESIDENCES

RES. RESIDENCES

GROUND FLOOR 1

9 MECH.
8 FACULTY OFFICES & SEM.
7 LABS
6 MAIN CONCOURSE
5 CLASSROOMS & LIBRARY
4 RESIDENCES & OFFICES

9 **8** **7** **6** **5** **4** **3** **1**

to hear and take part in discussions of law, medicine, philosophy, and through which they moved freely. Lethbridge was to be as open, as interchangeable and flexible as El Azhar, with neither walls nor partitions to impede interchange and interaction. The faculty's offices and the student residences were to be intermingled and interchangeable; everything that could be done physically to promote and facilitate interaction was to be done. But the sublimation of individual privacy—a professorial right manifest in the classroom and private office—to the ideal of openness was too much to expect, and the building as built provides a whole floor (the eighth) for faculty offices, and for the most part classes take place in classrooms with walls. Nevertheless, in what it does do, Lethbridge is a milestone.

The exterior of the building clearly and with great subtlety expresses the variety of functions that take place inside, using broad terms, not details, to do so. The long bands of concrete and glass on the upper levels vary in depth as the over-all function of each floor varies:

How do the Lethbridge students like living, sleeping, and eating, playing, studying and learning in the same building? Do they find the interaction, so much sought today, a real ingredient of university life as a result of having it all happen in the same place? Do they like the building?

The answer to all these questions is a strong "Yes". For one thing, they are not entirely confined to one building. There is now a Physical Education-Fine Arts building which attracts most students at one time or another, for athletics, art shows or classes, or drama. Also, a temporary building, moved from the community college site where the University began its existence, has been made into a pub. To reach these other buildings and the parking areas, a fiberglass tunnel from the Academic building winds up the hill to the Phys Ed building. Thus, students have reason and opportunity to leave the building. But there is academic, social and climatic convenience in "having it all happen" in one place: faculty members are easy to see and to meet; there is always someone to talk to and be with on the Concourse; and in Lethbridge's fairly rigorous climate—windy, snowy winters moderated by occasional warm Chinook winds, and quite hot summers—not to have to leave a weatherproof building is a real pleasure.

There are problems, of course, in the present isolation of the campus from the city, but these are not architectural, and the university will not always be so isolated. For the present, students without cars use the city bus service for transportation, and gradually are finding varieties of entertainment and stimulus on campus. As for the building, the students like it and are proud of it, whether or not they understand or are sensitive to the subtleties of its design and the grandeur of its concept.

Opposite the main entrance is a two story lounge (above) which opens out to the large terrace with its sculptural boiler stacks and spectacular view of the river valley. At one end of the lounge is the cafeteria; at the other, the lounge flows into the Concourse. The laboratory plan is based on the plan worked out for Scarborough College by Dr. W. E. Beckel, then dean of the College and now president of Lethbridge. These labs are more open than other instructional space: the corridor which is the seventh floor circulation runs along one side, a sometimes distracting but space-adding solution.

The main Concourse on the sixth floor is a main street for the whole university. It is the architectural statement of the "free exchange of ideas," the implementation of the goal of learning in places other than classrooms. There are always people on the Concourse, even in quiet periods. At class changes, and in the evening, it is even more like a street, full of students and faculty. Casual talk and informal meetings also happen on the Concourse, using the "platonic couches" (left and right: upholstered forms left from precasting of concrete for the building) which occur midway along the 912-foot long "street." Lighting throughout the building is indirect from recesses in the double-Tee beams. Nowhere is this more welcome than in the unbroken length of the concourse where fixtures would have been an interruption to the clear view from end to end. The floor is alternately concrete and carpet in gold with lines of yellow, tan and brown. Couches are yellow, chairs are upholstered in five colors coded to direct circulation, needed on so long a mall.

THE UNIVERSITY OF LETH-BRIDGE PROJECT ONE. Architects: Erickson-Massey Architects—Arthur Erickson, designer; Ron Bain, associate-in-charge; Gary Hanson, project architect; Robins Mitchell Watson, associated architects. Engineers: Bogue Babicki & Associates (structural); Ripley Klohn & Leonoff International Ltd. (foundation); Reid, Crowther & Partners Ltd. (mechanical/electrical). Consultants: Barron & Strachan (acoustical), William M.C. Lam & Associates (lighting), Erickson-Massey Architects (interiors), F.S. Dubin (mechanical), Poole Construction Ltd. (cost). Landscape architects: Erickson-Massey Architects. General contractor & construction manager: Poole Construction Ltd.

From every window on the east side of the building, and especially from the terrace, there is a view of the old Lethbridge Railway Bridge, a unique structure whose gossamer tracery makes a delicate web across the river valley. It stretches its flat length across the Oldman River like a horizon line and fits its supports into the banks and bed of the river. Visiting the site for the University for the first, time, Arthur Erickson was struck by the way in which the bridge used the terrain it had to cross and was deeply influenced in his design for the first building.

INTERIORS FOR WORSHIP

As a result of the Second Vatican Council and the liturgical study commissions it authorized, the Roman Catholic Church in 1969 issued a set of permanent guidelines for church design that have sharply modified the planning practice of centuries. To bring the priest nearer the congregation, the guidelines ordered the altar moved from its traditional backwall position to a more central location, with seating for the congregation ranged around—as in St. Thomas Aquinas (p. 69)—on three sides. This change permits the celebrant to face the congregation during the mass, simplifies the sightline and acoustical problems and allows the worshipper to feel more like a participant than a spectator. In many cases, altar rails are being dispensed with and organ lofts moved to positions nearer the altar. The emphasis on simplified ritual has eliminated many familiar devotional objects. Those that remain are treated as simple sculptural shapes, free of gilding or unnecessary ornament. New churches, as a result, have an uncluttered, contemporary appearance that, some Catholics complain, "makes them feel like Protestants."

A similar trend toward simplicity seems to be developing in temple and Protestant church design as well. We have been through a decade of unusual design freedom and church design continues to be near the poetic end of the design spectrum. But as churches of all faiths feel more competing claims on their funds, construction budgets are tightening. The First Christian Church of Kirksville, Missouri (p. 66) furnishes an excellent example of what strength, dignity and clarity of purpose can be achieved with an adequate but not indulgent design budget. Note the almost allegorical use of light and darkness.

One other emerging trend deserves notice. Because structures that get intensive use only one day per week are increasingly uneconomical to build and maintain, many new churches are being designed for wider community use. New weekday uses include concerts, dramas, craft workshops and sometimes drug clinics or special schools as the church tries to reshape its role in society and minister to Man's needs along a broader and more ecumenical front.

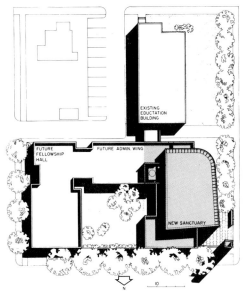

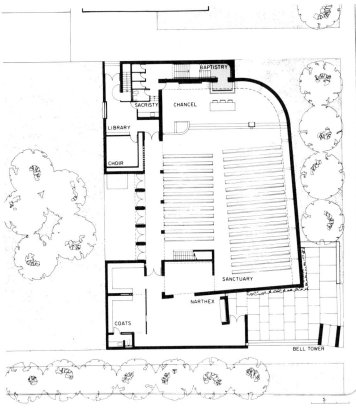

Materials for the church as a whole are dark brown face brick outside and on many surfaces inside, except the sanctuary, which is brick painted white. Ceilings are painted drywall and floors are concrete, with carpeting.

Robert Pettus photos

Careful control of light and form creates a spare setting for liturgical drama

Kirksville, Missouri is a town of 15,000 people about 200 miles from St. Louis. Like most small regional centers, its churches are an active part of community life; not only are there services and Sunday school, but pancake suppers, day care centers, Boy Scout meetings—and maybe even bingo games. The building of the new First Christian Church on these pages was an important event, and the architects—Anselevicius/ Rupe/Associates—quite naturally describe their design as a dialogue with the community as a whole. They have also dealt crea-

tively with the special liturgy of the church itself.

The entrance vestibule is low, with natural brick and soft browns to act in contrast to the main focus of the design, the sanctuary itself (opposite page). Here daylight streams in, the roof appears to float above the congregation, and the curved brick wall tries to avoid setting limits to the space. Anselevicius/Rupe have said the curved wall is one way of bringing the congregation in closer communion with themselves and with their minister, while still following a

basically basilican plan. The brick walls of the sanctuary are painted white as a further suggestion of unlimited space and inclusiveness.

In the Christian Church, each new member of the congregation is wholly immersed as a part of the baptismal ceremony, and the architects here have made that part of the liturgy an architectural event. Immersion takes place within the sanctuary, not behind it as in many Christian churches, and in the center of the chancel space. The people to be baptized first walk down into the

baptismal pool using the corridor behind the chancel, then out into the sanctuary through special doors behind the altar (see page 68). Plants have been set on the congregation side of the pool.

The subsidiary spaces of the new church expand the usefulness of the whole property. The major side aisle of the sanctuary has windows looking out on a garden, which will become a quiet and sheltered court yard when the future administration wing is built (see site plan). The sanctuary can be opened to the outside from this wall. The older education building is still in use on the site, and can be reached directly from the rear of the church. A coat room and a lavatory are located adjacent to the narthex, and can be converted into a bride's room by sliding doors.

FIRST CHRISTIAN CHURCH, Kirksville, Missouri. Architects: *Anselevicius/Rupe/Associates.—Charles R. Nash, project architect.* Structural engineers: *Thatcher and Patient, Inc.;* mechanical and electrical engineers: *Londe-Parker;* contractor: *Irvinbilt Co.*

The baptismal pool is placed behind the altar, and a white cross set in relief on the white brick wall completes the simple furniture of the chancel. When the baptismal pool is in use, the two doors (which help form a dramatic circle in the wall when closed) are opened to reveal the brick archway into the pool. The inside of these doors is painted a bright blue to match the blue behind the archway, forming a surprising new pattern on the white wall, as in the photo above.

A street in front of the church (photo, left) contrasts with the serenity of the interior.

Simplified but forceful design for a new Catholic worship

In the Church of St. Thomas Aquinas, in Indianapolis, the firm of Woollen Associates has responded to the architectural requirements of the simplified Roman Catholic liturgy with a design of great simplicity itself. The cross in the photograph above, for example, is the only one in the entire building. Nor will you see any devotional statues, softly flickering banks of votive candles, nor stained-glass windows. Gone is the romantic richness of architecture and decor, lovely and valid in its own day, but which properly belongs to eras now irrevocably dead. It has been replaced by a forthright-ness and strength of design that has an immense power all its own, and a 'message' in the language of today. The kaleidoscopic array of changing meanings which the architects' vibrant red design in-spires is also in keeping with the space itself. The stainless steel altar furnishings, designed by the firm, can be removed so that the great high space becomes a multi-purpose auditorium or theater.

The stimulus for the radically new and different kind of Catholic church architecture, of which St. Thomas Aquinas Church is an outstanding example, comes from outside the field of architecture itself. The broad aim of the Second Vatican Council was the modernization of the Church. In seeking to purify the liturgy, precepts were evolved which were aimed at giving back to the Mass more of the simplicity and spirit of the early Church. These precepts in turn were bound to drastically alter the layout and design of Catholic places of worship. The altar was made once again free-standing; the priest now faces the congregation gathered around it, all co-participants in the service, as opposed to the former long narrow nave arrangement where the average worshipper was perhaps too apt to think of himself as a spectator. In devising his own rendition of the new scheme, Woollen unabashedly borrows from modern theater design: the sanctuary becomes a thrust stage around which the congregation is arranged on a gently sloping incline in arc-like segments. The building itself is 'bent back' to greater than 180 degrees to further the idea of the altar as the center of a great circle. Another divider between priest and participants disappears with the absence of an altar rail. Worshippers now stand, rather than kneel, to receive Communion. "A church," Woollen said at the dedication ceremonies, "is a portrait of its people at a particular moment in time." Judged in these terms St. Thomas is as resoundingly successful in fulfilling its program as anything created during that age 'when the cathedrals were white.'

ST. THOMAS AQUINAS CHURCH, Indianapolis, Indiana. Architects: *Woollen Associates—Lynn Molzan, project architect;* engineers: *Fink, Roberts and Petrie, Inc. (structural); J. M. Rotz Engineering Co., Inc. (mechanical);* liturgical consultant: *Fr. Aiden Kavanaugh, O.S.B.;* acoustical consultant: *Dr. James Hyde.*

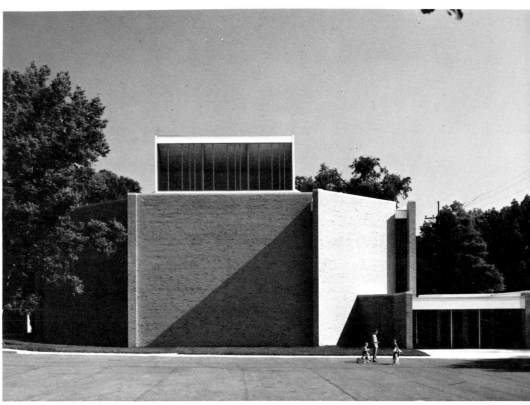

To the left of the sanctuary stands the Blessed Sacrament chapel, an intimate space for private worship. The rich purple wall ties in with the red of the cross but does not compete with it. Tabernacles formerly stood on the main altar, but are now once again placed in a separate area. The tabernacle's transparent sides and simple shape are perfectly in keeping with the church's bare block walls and exposed services and roof structure. The narthex, below left, contains the baptismal font and the penitent's entrance to the confessional. Stairs lead to a basement sacristy.

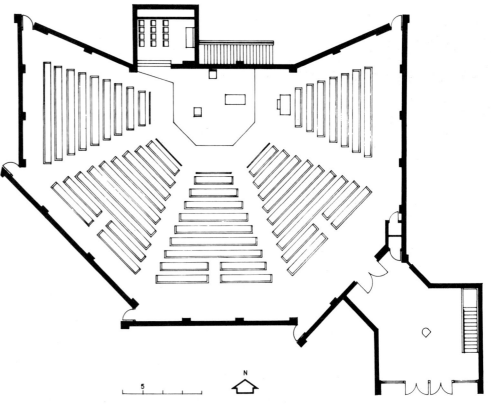

N

5

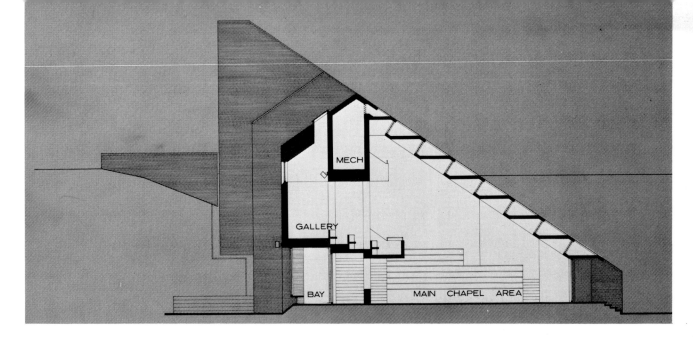

An exciting and strongly sculptured sanctuary with simple but rich details

Photos: Robert C. Lautman

In addition to its primary function, this campus chapel for a non-sectarian, junior college in Washington, D. C. serves as a setting for musical recitals, drama and a host of different student activities. Architects Hartman-Cox developed the chapel's complex, multi-level plan in response to a site that dips sharply toward the southeast and gave the structure a powerful roof form that follows the general slope of the site. The large interior volume, located at the lowest level in plan, is suffused with daylight, most of it reflected, for even the overhead clerestories admit little direct light and almost no sun.

The major materials inside are sand-finished plaster, white oak trim, vivid red carpet except on the floor of the main sanctuary where hardwood is used to reinforce sound. By breaking up the large expanses of wall and ceiling, acoustical problems that might otherwise have resulted were avoided and the architects were able to design a strongly sculptured enclosure for this exceptionally handsome devotional space.

CHAPEL, MT. VERNON COLLEGE, Washington, D.C. Architects: *Hartman-Cox*; engineers: *James M. Cutts* (structural); *JEK Associates* (mechanical); landscape architect: *Lester A. Collins*; contractor: *Edwin Davis.*

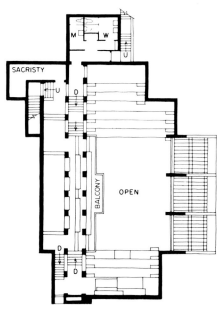

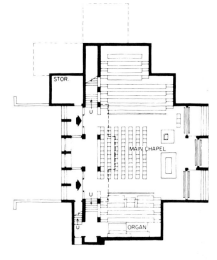

A spectacular volume, charged with color, for a Southern college congregation

The interior of Tuskegee Chapel is one of the most dramatic and powerful religious spaces to be built in this century. It is worth a pilgrimage to the school to see. Proud alumni are returning in increasing numbers to marvel at it, proving that it meets the ultimate criterion of a space for worship—that it have the power to evoke a universal response, rather than one limited to the esthetically trained.

One approaches the interior from humble spaces—up the stair near the meditation chapel, or from the modest narthex—and suddenly enters a great asymmetrical room. The ceiling is marvelous a great plane, curving in two directions, its warped surface formed by standard joists with straight bottom chords which appear to curve. The accordion-shaped plaster ceiling painted blue has been carefully engineered as a reflecting surface to enhance the acoustics. Air supply is equally distributed by means of brick-sheathed ducts on both sides of the chapel—handsome forms which complicate, yet enhance the interior space. Skylights parallel to the wall planes provide a mysterious and beautiful light.

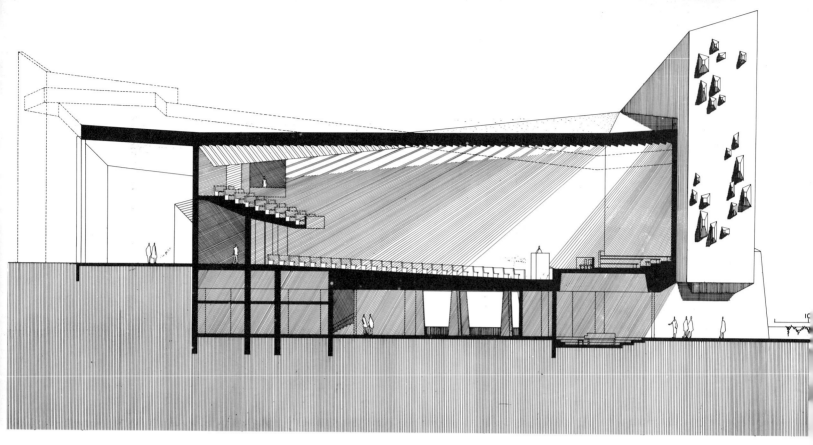

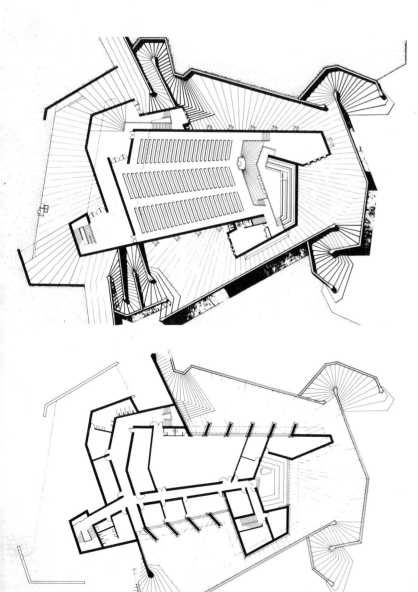

The chapel has been designed to function as a concert hall for the famous Tuskegee Institute Choir. The auxiliary spaces of the building will be used by the Tuskegee music school, until this entire sector of the campus becomes an art and music center, as part of Rudolph's new master plan for the campus.

The influence of Wright upon Rudolph is quite clear in this great room, but the architect appears to have drawn upon other sources including—unconsciously perhaps—certain images from German Expressionist films.

The views at the right are of the chancel, the lower photograph having been taken from the balcony. The chancel has been designed to emphasize the importance of the Tuskegee choir, and will eventually have an organ on the rear wall. The dominant position of the pulpit expresses the importance of the Word. A minister who has preched in this 1,100-seat chapel reports that from the pulpit it has a quality of intimacy and that the congregation seems near.

TUSKEGEE CHAPEL, Tuskegee Institute, Tuskegee, Alabama. Architects: *Fry & Welch, Architects & Planners;* associate architect (design phase): *Paul Rudolph;* architectural consultant for campus: *Moreland Griffith Smith;* structural engineer: *Donald J. Neubauer;* mechanical engineer: *A. Dee Counts;* electrical engineers: *Frank J. Sullivan Associates;* acoustical consultant: *Bolt Beranek and Newman;* contractors: *George B. H. Macomber Company and F. N. Thompson, Inc.*

Norman McGrath photos

A vigorous but simple statement for an urban, Orthodox community

The sanctuary of this new synagogue for an Orthodox
community evokes a warm and sensitive religious ambience
by simple, yet powerful, architectural means. It is on a
limited site closely flanked by a tall apartment house
and two-family residences, which precluded any effective
use of side windows. Top lighting which plays on the
undulations and curves of the interior walls provides
not only an apt solution to the problem, but has been
developed into the major design feature of the space.
The skylights, fitted with artificial lights as well,
are concealed by a sculptured plaster ceiling molded
to give form and scale to the room, and by deep,
slanted wells acting as a cut-off for the lights.
In addition to those ranging the side walls, two larger
ones in the middle focus light and attention on the
centrally placed Bema and on the concave shaped Ark

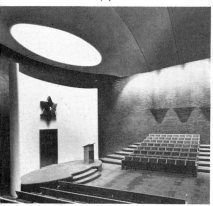

wall where such significant
symbols as the Ark, Eternal
Light, and Star of David
read as isolated elements
on the white plaster surface.
Richard Foster chose an
interesting ironspot brick
for the interior and the
exterior because of its
self-cleaning quality, the
depth of coloration, and the
ease of obtaining the various
required shapes. Stone, where
used, is red sandstone and
the ornamental metal work is black anodized aluminum. The
contractor was Herbert Construction Co.; engineers were
Zoldos and Meagher (structural) and Meyer, Strong & Jones
(mechanical); consultants were Emil Antonucce (sculpture
and graphics); Ranger Farrell & Associates (acoustics) and
Richard Kelly and John L. Kilpatrick (lighting).

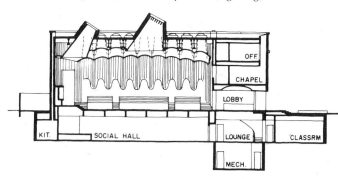

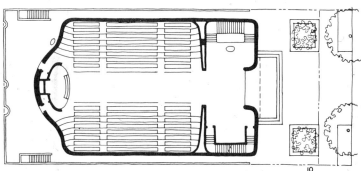

Two congregations
in Memphis
share a dramatic,
evocative synagogue

Two Memphis congregations commissioned architects Francis Mah and Walk Jones to design a single synagogue as a center for their joint worship. Major elements in the design are a large sanctuary, a small chapel and an expansive social hall which occasionally serves both the sanctuary and the chapel as overflow space. The design for each grew out of a regularized structural system that included long bands of daylight from clerestories along transverse column lines (see plan). In the vestibule and chapel (photos, lower left), this overhead light source is a primary design tool.

The horseshoe-shaped main sanctuary is emotive and highly charged with drama. Its appeal is directly to our senses and to the emotions these senses inspire. Ranks of silver-colored, acoustical baffles hang in concentric rows from the ceiling or march in a steady cadence around the curving rear wall. Lights from sources seen and unseen pick up the colors of chair and carpet and reflect these colors from every surface. The whole interior seems suffused with color.

This arresting space, too theatrical perhaps for some, reaffirms for all how potent is interior architecture's capacity to communicate.

ANSHEI-SPHARD/BETH EL EMETH SYNAGOGUE, Memphis, Tennessee. Architects: *Mah + Jones, Inc.;* engineers: *Ellers Reaves Fanning and Oakley, Inc.* (mechanical and electrical); *Wooten-Smith & Weiss* (structural); contractor: *Grinder, Taber and Grinder, Inc.*

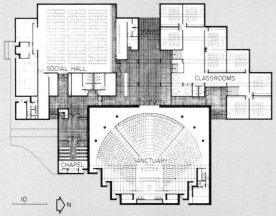

SOCIAL HALL
CLASSROOMS
CHAPEL
SANCTUARY
10 N

Otto Baitz photos

Bold structural forms create a contemporary church for a traditional monastic order

The new church is sited on rolling land which overlooks Benet Lake. The main sanctuary seats 300 laymen with choir stalls for a maximum of 36 monks. The altar is at the far end, although the plan would also function well if the altar were at the center. The church serves as a principal entry to the monastery proper. Access to and from the monastery is by means of a double ramp and connecting corridor which passes through the exposed concrete wedge-shaped link, passing under the hollow cylinder in which the bell is hung.

The plan provides for two different kinds of ceremonial processions, and its two major axes form a cross which is expressed in the roof truss system as well as the plan.

No actual Cross appears on the church exterior, but one of rusted metal, made by a member of the Order is placed near the entrance. Tigerman intended his building to resemble a church only in the sense that it functions as a church. By avoiding a linear hierarchic plan with an overwhelmingly dominant axis he created a more intimate space that tends to surround and embrace the congregation. The plan shape encourages active community and lay participation in the service.

The church is basically a 68-foot square concrete box concealed by an 8-foot-wide sloping earth berm. The geometrically ingenious roof is not as complex as it appears at first glance. It consists of ten simple trusses of laminated beechwood. Tigerman has created his sloping planes by leaving out the top horizontal chords of the perimeter trusses as the diagram (lower right) indicates. The vertical planes on the perimeter are surfaced in metal. The others are glazed with solar bronze glass forming clerestories which dramatically light the main sanctuary. The interior of the church is as simple and direct in its juxtaposition of functional elements and its use and joining of materials as is the exterior. The connecting bridge from the monastery appears in the three photos p. 84. Like the double ramp to which it connects, it is emphatically separated from the adjacent exposed concrete walls. These walls thus appear as continuous surfaces which adjoin the remaining walls of the sanctuary to form one unbroken concrete envelope. The ceiling is sharply defined from the walls by the straightforward use of beechwood trusses and interior decking, as well as by the solar glass. Even the carpet has its own clearly articulated edge.

The total cost of the church including site work, landscaping and a new road was $340,000. The per square foot cost was $37.98 for a total of 8,950 square feet. The principal structural materials are exposed and no veneers or facings have been used. Since the bulk of the building has been constructed below ground, heat loss or gain is minimized and energy thus conserved.

ST. BENEDICT'S ABBEY CHURCH, Benet Lake, Wisconsin. Owner: *The Benedictine Fathers.* Architects: *Stanley Tigerman of Stanley Tigerman & Associates* —associates: *John F. Fleming and Anthony Saifuku;* engineers: *The Engineers Collaborative* (structural); *Walter Flood & Company* (foundation and soils); *Wallace & Migdal* (mechanical and electrical); general contractor: *Pepper Construction Company.*

Robert Lautman photos

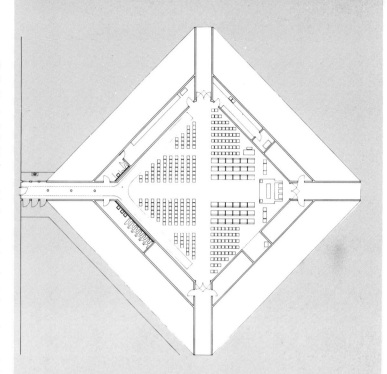

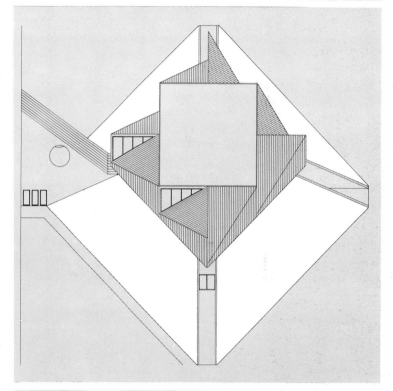

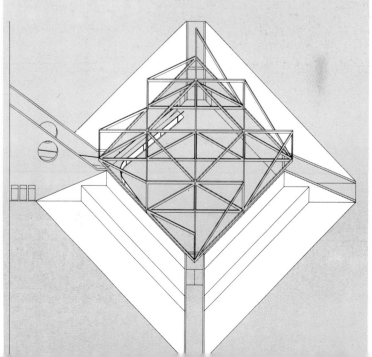

The masonry bridge enters at the upper level on one of the two long axes and frames the altar in a head-long view. From this entry point, parishioners make their way to the floor seating by means of a pair of inclined concrete ramps.

A little-used parish house in Washington, D.C. becomes a beautiful small chapel

This small chapel has been shaped from a two-story parish house that formed an annex to a nineteenth-century Episcopal church. Much of the success of the renovation stems from architect Philip Ives' decision to move the choir practice room upstairs and slope its floor upward at both ends to gain space in the chapel below (see section). The added height in the chapel is used at the rear for a row of overhead organ pipes and, behind the altar, for a high wall washed by concealed lighting. The effective use of light as a design tool, the simple but elegant detailing and the careful choice of finish materials combine to form a very handsome and exceptionally successful renovation.

Interior walls are textured plaster, floors are gray slate, woodwork is stained dark. Chairs, altar, lectern and font are designed by the architect.

CHAPEL OF ST. JUDE, CHRIST CHURCH, Washington, D.C. Architect: *Philip Ives;* associate architect: *Theo Dominick;* structural engineer: *Carl C. Hanson;* mechanical engineer: *William A. Brown;* landscape architect: *Peter C. Rolland;* lighting consultant: *Edison Price;* contractor: *E. A. Baker Company.*

Robert C. Lautman photos

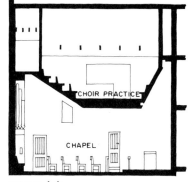

SECTION A-A

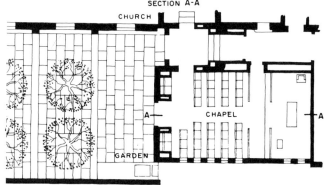

85

INTERIORS FOR BUSINESS

It is not an accident that the rise of corporate values in business corresponds historically to the advent of the contemporary skyscraper in American cities. Nor is it by chance that the office tower became the manifest symbol of those values. The tower, after all, gives ample opportunity for the vertical expression of hierarchical values and the cellular construction of modern steel frame office buildings is perfectly suited for establishing and maintaining precedence. So well mated are these two, that each is mutually reinforcing and each works toward the preservation of the other. But by the mid 1960s, many people outside those towers were already questioning these corporate values, and many inside were noticing that precedence has little to do with day to day business operations. In fact, it sometimes hindered those operations by physically separating people at different levels in the corporation who needed to work most closely together. The "office landscape" was one result and perhaps the most promising since it could function in the kinds of spaces produced in speculative office buildings. By relating workers efficiently and by removing the barriers to easy communication, office planners have produced a much more fluid ambience for work, but many problems remain only partially solved. Of these, the visual and the acoustic are the most vexing. The three-quarter height partitions that most "landscape" plans employ produce a chaotic and bewildering array of tiny cubicles with unclear routes for circulation in between. And the requirements for sound absorptive materials are excessive. Even when these materials are in place, many installations require special sound masking devices or "acoustical perfume". The most successful installations to date seem to be those like the Commerce Clearing House by Marquis & Stoller (page 123) which blend office landscape with certain elements of traditional office layout.

Other factors have been at work to reshape our offices. The need for duplicating, computing and communications equipment on a new scale has made heavy spatial demands—demands which architects and manufacturers have been meeting with increasing skill. Finally, there is a new work ethic emerging as a result of shifting public attitudes toward work itself. Our image of work—particularly office work—is becoming more relaxed, more compatible with beards, long hair, individual initiative and expression. The informality of many of the offices in this section reflect this new and liberating ethic.

Bold structural forms reinforce a research firm's corporate identity

Viewed from almost any vantage point, Burroughs-Wellcome is a large and complex structure. It encloses some 300,000 square feet of laboratory and administrative space distributed unevenly over five stories. In plan, the building forms a giant "S" with opposing arms that embrace a main entry court and a large service yard. Reception, cafeteria, library, auditorium and administrative offices flank the entry court. Laboratories, research offices and quarters for test animals surround the service yard.

Flexibility was a primary programmatic goal. Each major area in Rudolph's plan—laboratories, administration and support services—can be expanded by simple, linear addition. To prepare for this eventuality, the architect left the expansible ends of the building expressed in a somewhat random pattern of flattened hexagons. Any of the elements can be extended horizontally without disturbing the building's visual order. This device, combined with an elaborate articulation of parts, complicates the elevations considerably but gives the building an agreeable scale and plunges it squarely into the realm of dynamic architectural sculpture. The complications of the exterior assert themselves inside with no less force. The three-story lobby space closes dramatically overhead in a turbulent and visually compelling spatial composition. The administrative offices are shaped at the exterior wall to receive skylights that admit daylight from an unseen and unexpected source. The board room, over the cafeteria, opens out through a canted window wall to one of the fairest scenes in North Carolina: a timbered Piedmont plain with the spires of Chapel Hill in the distance.

Throughout the building, the inclined columns seem to emerge, disappear and re-emerge freely. When they lie in the plane of a wall, they are simply integrated without fussy detail. When they stand independently, the space flows around them with only the merest hint of obstruction. Diagonal relationships are present everywhere and right-angled elements, when they appear, do so almost apologetically. The spaces are particularized and personal; as much the opposite of universal space as Rudolph could make them. A simple and consistent vocabulary of finishes gives the administrative areas an easy continuity and flow.

The Burroughs-Wellcome building is not for those who are disturbed by departures from the norm. The sharp-eyed visitor may find details that are not completely resolved. But if there is bravura here, it is more than balanced by solid accomplishment. The building is functional—probably no more and no less so than similar facilities of more routine design. What is best about Burroughs-Wellcome is the sense of exhilaration and spatial excitement it awakens.

Joseph W. Molitor photos

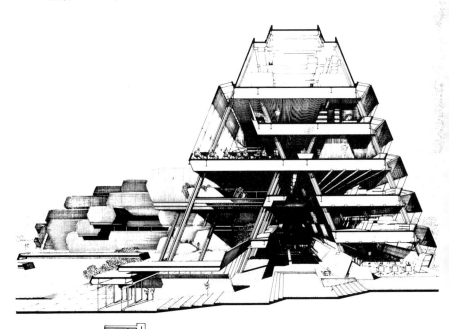

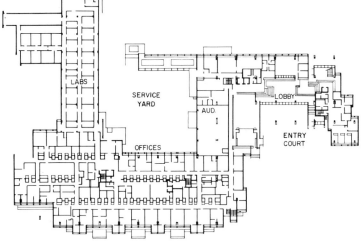

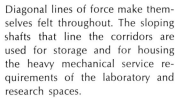

Diagonal lines of force make themselves felt throughout. The sloping shafts that line the corridors are used for storage and for housing the heavy mechanical service requirements of the laboratory and research spaces.

BURROUGHS-WELLCOME CO., Research Triangle Park, North Carolina. Architect: *Paul Rudolph*; engineers: *Lockwood-Greene Engineers*, Inc.; contractor: *Daniel Construction Co.*

New life for an aging warehouse on San Francisco's reviving waterfront

Along with a number of other groups in San Francisco, when Dancer-Fitzgerald-Sample, Inc. decided to find new office space in 1968, they took a close look at the old warehouses along the now drowsy North Waterfront. When the architects, R. A. Zambrano and Gwin Richards of the Hugh Stubbins/Rex Allen Partnership, told DFS that the 1907 structure they had tentatively selected was sound, they plunged into the remodeling with the vigor that only an advertising agency could muster. Selecting a building committee with representatives from all the departments, including the secretaries, they began to study the problem. Even though they admit in retrospect that the architect's recommendations were always the best ones in the end, the committee analyzed everything from building procedures to fabric and color choices. Two principal design problems had to be solved; first, the arrangement of necessary work spaces on the second floor which, at the same time, would preserve everyone's view of the existing timber trusses; and second, an entrance and main stairway that would draw visitors to the second floor from the street with as little effort and as much drama as possible. The photographs see above right and the photos following show how handsomely the criteria were met. Starting with straightforward loft space, (below right) the client and architect placed most of the private offices around the perimeter. All are roofless so that the structure can be seen above. The inviting entrance, (that) visible through the arched facade from the street, focuses on a reception desk that is halfway to the second floor. Views up into the vaulted space from that point, (next page), tie the two parts of the design firmly together. Engineers: *Geoffrey Barrett*, structural; *O'Kelly and Schoenlank*, mechanical; *Mel Cammissa*, electrical. Contractor: *Robert L. Wilson, Inc.*

Sloping-walled offices, above, are open to the trussed space but have curtains for visual privacy. The bridge, (right), connects a glass-walled conference room with the offices.

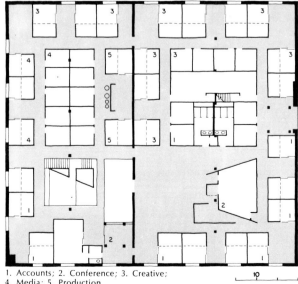

1. Accounts; 2. Conference; 3. Creative;
4. Media; 5. Production

Ernest Braun photos

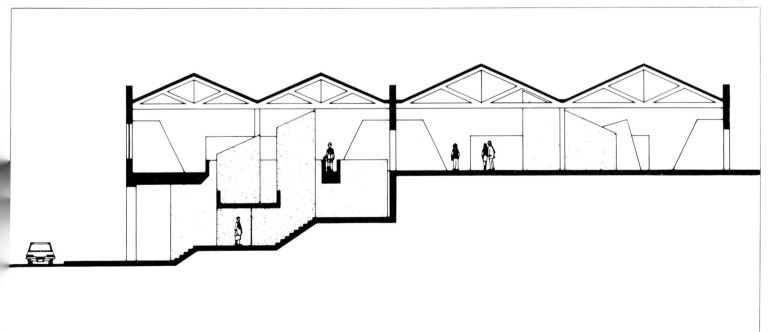

Alexandre Georges photos

Renovated headquarters
for an avant garde publisher
in New York's Greenwich Village

Since its establishment in 1951, Grove Press has outgrown a series of Manhattan offices. The firm now occupies space in a newly renovated building in Greenwich Village—a section of the city long associated with artists and writers. For the publishers of *The Evergreen Review,* (and first in the U. S. to publish Henry Miller, William Burroughs and D. H. Lawrence) these new interiors had to reflect an avant-garde spirit without sacrifice to efficient, comfortable, working surroundings.

The renovation was carried out by two wholly-owned Heery & Heery subsidiaries: Interiors for Business Inc. and Design Directions who combined to plan and complete the renovation in just seven months. Using conventional materials, inventive graphics and furnishings, many of which are modern classics, the designers have created a series of vital, fresh and expressive spaces. Heery & Heery, *Architects.* Mechanical and electrical engineers: *S. A. Bogen & Associates.*

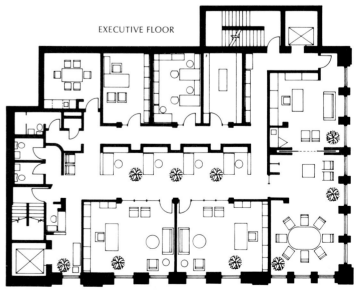

EXECUTIVE FLOOR

Lawrence S. Williams, Inc. photos

A bank for passenger-depositors in the holding lounge of the Philadelphia Airport

This branch office of a Philadelphia bank is located in a passenger waiting area of the city's international airport. Working with few materials but using them splendidly, the designers have created a tranquil pocket amid otherwise busy surroundings.

The gently vaulted ceiling of oiled cherrywood strips hangs effortlessly over the space and unifies it. Banking counters and half-height partitions in the same material are detailed with exemplary care. End walls are covered in champagne-colored vinyl and the carpeting is Moroccan red.

Shunning supergraphics or other modish expression, the design has a restraint and timeless excellence that does credit to both the architect and his client. Vincent Kling, *Architect.* Mechanical and electrical engineer: *A. E. D'Ambly;* contractor: *Interior Milling Co.*

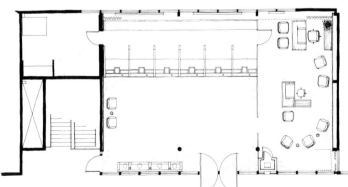

Reflective surfaces and bright colors give sparkle to a downtown ticket office

Morley Baer photos

Part of a major renovation of United Airlines' four-story building in San Francisco, this showcase ticket office opens across a busy intersection toward Union Square. Architects Arthur Gensler & Associates turned the axis of the ticket lobby on the diagonal to face the square. From this decision, others followed directly. The enclosing glass wall was kept free of the exterior column line and allowed to step in and out, creating a series of small bays and considerable visual interest. The diagonal axis is strongly re-emphasized in the ticket counters, the lighting coffers over the counters and the saw-toothed wall behind.

Bright primary colors and sparkling interior finishes generate enormous excitement. Floors are dark brick, partitions are plasterboard, counters are covered in plastic laminate and columns are clad in polished stainless steel to reduce their bulk and reflect the movement and color within the space. A white-on-white relief, displaying the United Airlines logo along with the principal cities served, forms a spirited and strongly textured end wall.

UNITED AIRLINES TICKET OFFICE, San Francisco, California. Architects: *M. Arthur Gensler & Associates (Don Kennedy, project architect)*; structural engineers: *Forell-Elsesser-Chan*; mechanical engineers: *Higash & Associates*; electrical engineers: *Shinn & Associates*; contractor: *Arthur Brothers, Inc.*

Free-standing trading desks open the entire space of a Rochester brokerage house

In order to eliminate the typical "back room" in a brokerage office, the order room, in this design by Booth and Nagle of Chicago for the Rochester office of Shearson-Hammill Co., Inc., which serves all brokers and customers, has a central place, (right). To capitalize on a space unbroken by columns, the architects have designed, in collaboration with the Cambridge Seven Associates, a four-person trading desk that allows brokers to share equipment and secretarial services. The diagonal placement of the desks emphasizes the openness of the room, allows easy movement from desk to desk and permits flexibility in office organization. The rounded corners on the panels separating desks, right, are meant, says Jim Nagle, to complement the flowing space. Surfaces are black plastic with oak trim, and chrome hardware.

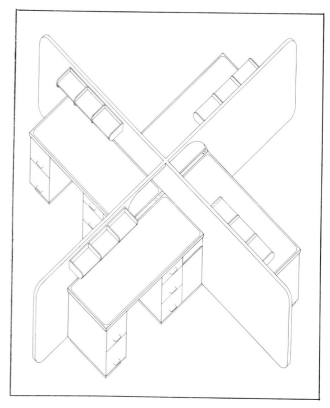

Hedrich-Blessing photo

**Equal doses of color
and whimsey
attract customers to
this smart beauty parlor**

TINTING

SHAMPOO

DRIERS

VIP

HAIR
STYLERS

RECEPT.

MEN'S
BOUTIQUE

5

Verve and a good dash of supergraphic color give strong identity to this otherwise trim and functionally designed beauty parlor and men's boutique. The idea of combining the two types of shops is to get the women to buy presents for their husbands after having their hair done. The basic finishes and fittings are white: painted walls, vinyl floors, vinyl chair covering and plastic laminate cabinets. Color is concentrated at the entrance, accent floor inlays around chairs and in silhouette fin-walls. The shop is by Design Coalition/Alan Buchsbaum, architect; Alan Mitelman, graphic designer. The contractor was John Blom.

Norman McGrath photos

ALCAN's Toronto offices sparkle with aluminum and inventive lighting

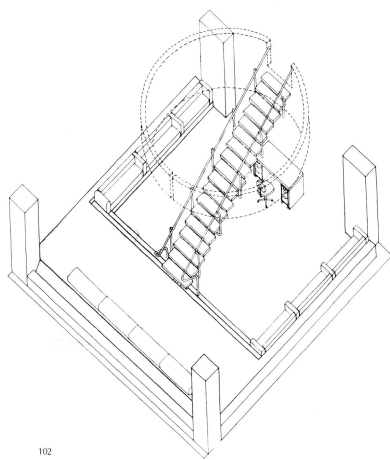

The elevator lobby and reception area for the Toronto offices of Aluminum Company of Canada, Ltd., (color photo, above, and opposite) establish the major visual impact of the offices for a visitor. Neon tubes at the ceiling lead from the elevator space of both floors into the reception area, acting as a strong visual magnet pulling the visitor along. The reception area occupies both floors (see plan, page 105) with a spectacularly open, carpeted aluminum stair rising through the center of a full circle cut in the framing of the 21st floor.

The building in which these spaces are leased is Mies van der Rohe's 56-story Toronto Dominion Centre (RECORD, March 1971, pages 105-114). ALCAN houses about 140 people —including 87 executives—on both floors. A majority of perimeter wall space is thus occupied by private offices, but one of the major objectives of the design was to give secretarial and clerical employees direct outside light, too. The intermittent secretarial bays (see plans, and photo, page 105) accomplish this, and eliminate any large, impersonal secretarial pools. The main circulation path around the building's core is more a gallery than a corridor (photo, page 105). It is a full seven feet wide, it has exposed incandescent lighting fixtures that cause high contrast and "sparkle" off the silvery glass finishes, and there

are built-in filing and coat clos-
ets along its length to further
mix the use of the space.

The plan and section of the
reception and elevator areas (p.
105) help explain the arrangements for neon tubing, so dominant in many of these photographs. One tube leads from
each of eight elevator doors,
running parallel to each other
down the corridor and converg-
ing on the aluminum-clad circular passage between floors. At
this point the tubes turn 90 degrees vertically, and run around
the circular opening in both directions. It is a dramatic display
of lighting, and a dramatic initial
representation of ALCAN's offices.

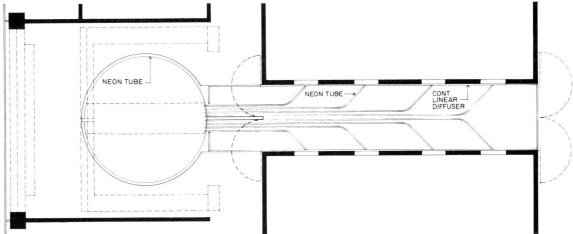

REFLECTED CEILING PLAN-20TH FLOOR

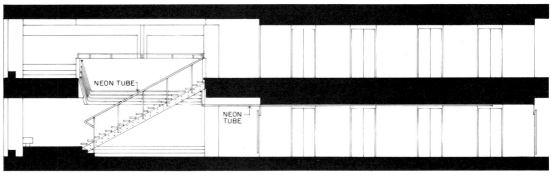

LONGITUDINAL SECTION

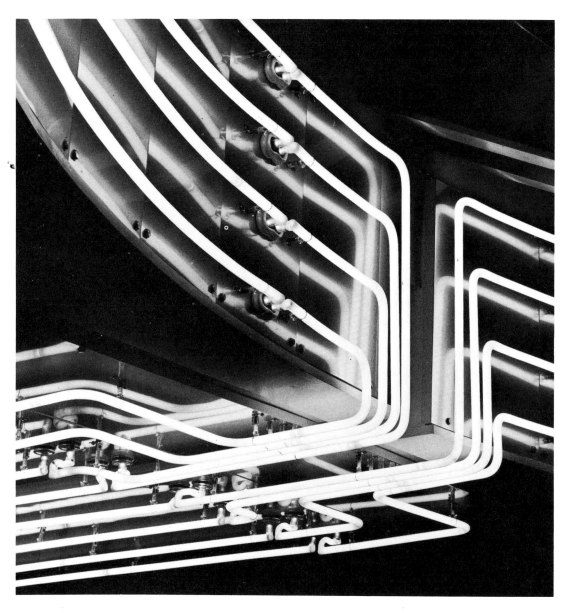

Aluminum-like finishes have been used in many areas of the office, like the planter tubes in the photos below, built-in closet doors, and the cube office tables designed by the architects, shown in the photo at right. The ceilings throughout both floors are those provided by the office building.

All of the walls of the ALCAN floors in the plans (p. 105) are metal studs and gypsum board, fixed in place. The designers spent extra money making floor-to-ceiling glass walls in front, allowing indirect light inside. Curtains may be drawn in any office for privacy, while the relatively mullion free secretarial bays create a spacious, elegant mood.

ALCAN CORPORATE OFFICES, Toronto, Canada. Architects: *A. J. Diamond & Barton Myers—A. J. Diamond, Barton Myers & Tony Marsh, design team.* Cost control: *Helyar, Vermeulen, Rae & Mauchan;* mechanical & electrical engineers: *H. H. Angus Associates;* structural engineers: *C. D. Carruthers & Wallace;* general contractors: *McMullen & Warnock Ltd.*

Ian Samson photos

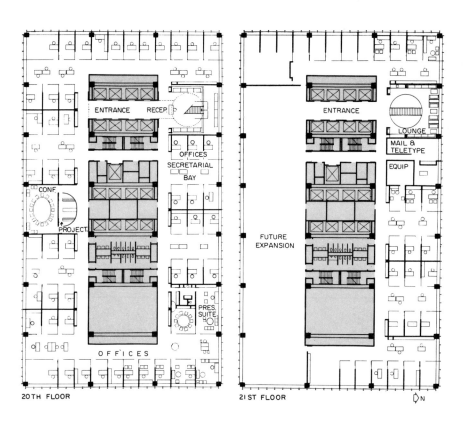

ENTRANCE   RECEP.

OFFICES

SECRETARIAL
BAY

CONF

PROJECT.

PRES.
SUITE

O F F I C E S

20TH FLOOR

ENTRANCE

LOUNGE

MAIL &
TELETYPE

EQUIP

FUTURE
EXPANSION

21ST FLOOR   N

A voluptuously sculptured stair creates a glamorous environment for haute coiffure

As part of the renovation of York Square, an old three-story house has become the luxurious Vidal Sassoon Salon in Toronto. Architects A. J. Diamond and Barton Myers, working with Barrie Briscoe on graphics and Muller & Stewart on furniture, have used a free-standing staircase in a semi-circular, sky-lit well to tie all the floors together. The ground floor has two entrances, one from York Square, and serves as a reception area and boutique, (below). On a mezzanine added by the architects, half a flight up, are the dressing rooms. Next floor in ascending order of privacy and function is cutting and shampoo, (left), and at the top, closest to the sky-light are the stations for tinting and wig fitting, (opposite page). Engineers: *M. S. Yolles and Associates,* structural; *Rybka, Smith & Ginsler,* mechanical; owner and contractor: *Iaver Investments, Ltd.*

Ian Samson photos

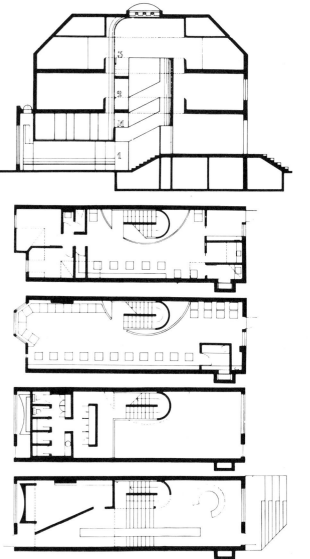

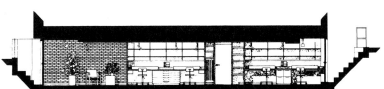

Throwaway space in a Baltimore brownstone is salvaged to create a small office for young architects

Pursuing a search for inexpensive space, three architects who are opening their own practice found an unused service corridor in a hundred-year-old Baltimore brownstone. Six-and-one-half-feet-wide and seven steps below sidewalk level, awkwardly proportioned and badly deteriorated, with little light and no heat, the space seemed to have nothing much to recommend it.

But from this bleak beginning, the architects fashioned an exceptionally pleasant work space. They removed the old plaster and painted the exposed brick white. They installed a new plaster board ceiling and new doors and sidelights front and rear. They laid a new floor of 1 by 6 pine planks using chipped stone at the entry and as infill between the pilasters. Drafting positions were built-in along one wall and separated with light wood partitions. Lighting tracks were mounted overhead to serve both the drafting areas and the display boards behind.

The final result is a very handsome small office. But more than that, it is an office imaginatively redeemed on a rock bottom budget from the city's growing inventory of throwaway space. *The Design Collaborative* Architects, Baltimore, Maryland. Contractor: *Valley Construction Co.*

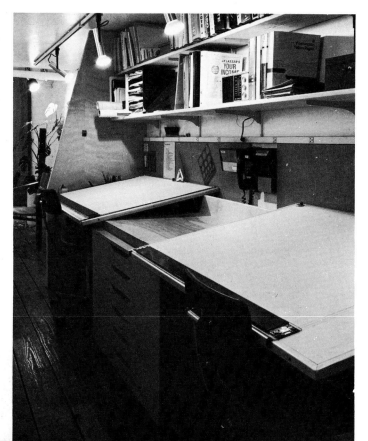

John Whitehall photos

The allocation of space was governed in large part by the exigencies of structure. A pair of column lines (see plan) suggested the development of windowed drafting carrels along the outside walls and the central floor area was then available for files and general reference. The total floor area is approximately 1,400 square feet with a personnel capacity of twelve.

From barn to architect's office an easy and convincing transition

In converting the upper level to their own use, the architects retained the main structural framing including 6-by-6 wood columns and main carrier beams, knee-braced and joined by wood-dowelled mortise and tenon connections. New window openings were cut to fit between the main structural members. The remaining wall and ceiling surfaces were insulated and covered with white tackboard. Floors were carpeted and indirect lighting was introduced in the form of mercury vapor lamps turned upward toward the ceiling. Drafting tables and reference desks were designed by the architects. Toilets, kitchenette, conference room and reception area were provided in a single addition when the architects moved in.

Roth and Saad have a general practice. Saad explains, "We want to be regarded as good thinkers, not specialists in one building form or another." This concern, perhaps implicit in the choice of an old barn over more orthodox rental space, is clearly expressed in the simple but imaginative way that the practical problems of restoration and conversion have been confronted, studied and solved.

Robert Perron photos

OFFICE OF HAROLD ROTH-EDWARD SAAD, Hamden, Connecticut. Architects: *Roth and Saad;* mechanical engineers: *Hubbard, Lawless & Osborne Associates Inc.;* lighting consultants: *Sylvan R. Shemitz & Associates;* contractor: *Donovan Brothers.*

Cheerful surroundings
ease patients' anxieties

Located in an apartment house, this lively dental office makes maximum use of minimum space. Services are collected along one wet wall and, in accordance with current practice, operating rooms are screened from the waiting room by a sliding door. The nurse's station, designed by the architect, is centrally located for visual control. Because many of the patients are youngsters, the architects have selected materials that are durable and easily maintained—vinyl for wall coverings and plastic laminate for counters.

The sparkling overhead lighting and the warm, ingratiating color scheme invest this windowless waiting room with a special cheerfulness that acts to ease patients' anxieties. *Smith & Munter*, Architects. Mechanical engineer: *Seymour Berkowitz*; contractor: *Sam Amato*.

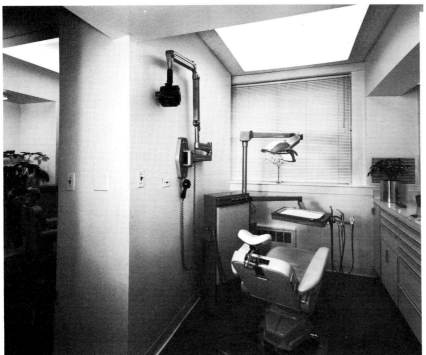

James Brett photos

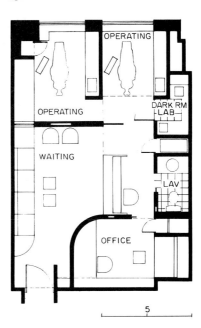

5

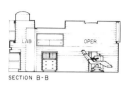

SECTION A-A

SECTION B-B

Wayne Thom photos

Open operatory and residential character are reassuring to patients

The clear-span operatory in these offices provides open, lounge-like space for the three dental chairs ranged along one wall facing a window, and the built-in cabinets and work counter along the opposite wall. This individualized plan provides the orthodontist-tenant with free and flexible space, in which he and his assistant can work, and a pleasant, almost residential environment for the patients, most of whom are children and young adolescents, for whom the warm redwood walls, the bright colors of the cabinets and equipment, and the general lighting are reassuring. The informality of the open operatory, with no screens or partitions between dental chairs, is an added form of reassurance. General, rather than local, lighting was the client's choice and a combination of artificial (ceiling mounted fluorescent strip fixtures above the dental chairs) and natural (from the high window, louvered for control) provides the desired amount of light. The architects designed all the built-in furnishings (reception desk and magazine rack, instrument and supply cabinets, "equipment module" by each chair).

ORTHODONTIST'S OFFICE for Dr. Edward D. Givins, Redondo Beach, California. Architects: *Black, Pagliuso, Kikuchi and O'Dowd; Peter C. Boccato,* job captain. Contractor: *Joe Baune.*

Karl Sliva

Common components and legible spaces mark Toronto's Medical Association Building

A quiet Toronto street in one of the city's older residential sections has a new office building on it, housing the headquarters facilities for the Ontario Medical Association, and the building may be a little puzzling to any of the neighborhood people who have seen it both inside and out. The street facade is simple, almost conservative and haphazard in its flatness, with its simple punched holes for large windows that are in nearly the same plane as the brick, and with two large openings at either end of the building that obviously lead up from and down to a parking garage below. Though there are details around the entrance that tell a trained eye (or an architect) that the intentions of the designers here were serious, complex, and probably meant as a challenge, still

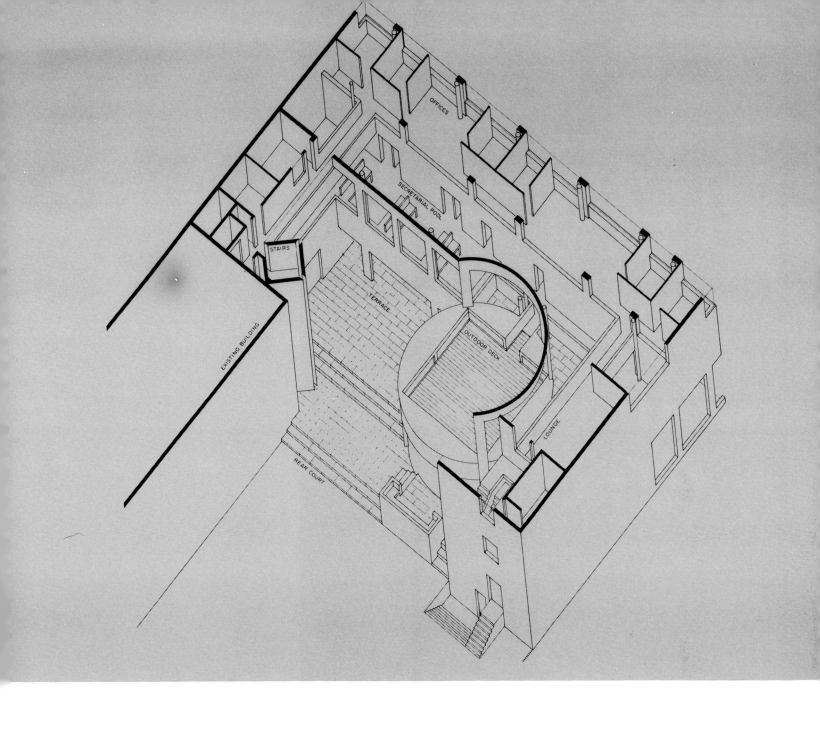

the effect of the street facade is quite unremarkable. But the effect of the inside spaces, as in the photo at left, is not. Walls rise through three floors with clerestory lighting at the top, exterior light is brought through two separated planes of glass causing the darker interior glass to reflect the image of the lighter exterior walls, and common electrical ducts are exposed on the wall surfaces along with their outlet boxes and warm and cold air piping. It is the combination of "averageness" on the facade, the spectacular display of spatial gymnastics inside, and the use of usually concealed ducts as decoration that would be surprising to any layman.

To the architects A. J. Diamond and Barton Myers, of course, it is an expression of their convictions re-

garding architecture, and what they believe should be made important in their buildings. Both architects worked in the office of Louis Kahn, and they both acknowledge the influence on them of Robert Venturi's ideas. They have not been interested in elaborated structure—in exposing the bones of their buildings—but they have been concerned with expressing the activities of people. They say about the O.M.A. Building: "Instead of expending funds and energy on 'architecture' which in truth often means structural exhibitionism, or conspicuously expensive finishes, or excessive 'articulation', judgments made were in reference to the importance of activities, and user work requirements." The three principal activities within the O.M.A. are the

administrative functions of the permanent staff, the executive function, which is carried out periodically (at least once every month) by meetings of the board of representatives, and the entertainment, dining and social functions of the association.

It is easy to see from the plans (page 115) which of these functions has been given symbolic emphasis over the others, and to understand why. The board meetings, at which decisions are made regarding the daily operations and ultimate public values of the Ontario medical profession, are the raison d'etre of the O.M.A. itself, and the board room has thus been made the center of attention of the whole design. It is circular where the rest of the spaces are rectilinear, and it is one of the largest

spaces in plan, much larger than its programmed 40-person seating capacity might require. It exudes a kind of elegance (page 117) that the rest of the building has tried to avoid.

The other two activities interlock spatially throughout the rest of the building: the areas available for entertainment and public functions are on the ground floor, and executive or administrative functions occur on the upper two floors. The main lounge on the first floor (photo pp. 114-115) is near the entrance for large public dinners or receptions, the employees may use it during the working day and at lunch, and it is immediately available before board meetings. The major space of the administrative area is the secretarial pool on the second floor (photo, page 116). It rises

through two floors, acknowledging its use by the largest daily concentrations of people, and the low-ceilinged one- and two-man offices surround the secretarial area on two floors. Finally, these activities are linked through three floors by the interior open space around the board room; the curved wall of the board room is visible from all floors and is the architectural event by which visual orientation is possible from any other place in the building.

The interior feeling of most of the O.M.A. Building is one of casualness. Except for the board room there is a kind of studied devaluation of hierarchies which is implied by the spatial interlocking of activities just described. But it is easy to notice Diamond's and Meyers' other efforts

to make the building unpretentious and to relax it: such information is supplied most clearly by the detailing; the selection of fixtures and finishes, and the small parts of the building chosen for emphasis. The cold and warm air ducts of the mechanical system are directly exposed to view, and sometimes used as sculpture in space, as with the ductwork (see page 117) leading from the entrance foyer to the conference room. The ducts are common spiral tubing of galvanized steel with the usual flexible elbows of aluminum, all with a white enamel finish baked on before installation. There are chromed splicing straps at each joint and chromed hangers. Their impact lies in their obvious commonness—even laymen know these things are usually hidden

in basements or ceilings—and in their formal organization. The same judgments apply to the common tubing used as handrails, and to the lighting—ordinary flexible conduit and four-way outlet boxes have been exposed throughout the building in expressive ways.

The O.M.A. building's emphasis on the expression of human activities, and the architects' lack of commitment to any basic structural clarity certainly add up to a kind of devaluation of technological issues; the architecture doesn't much exhibit a concern for technical expression or even of rationalism, with its usual scientific emphasis. A kind of technical rationalism has always been one of the firmest foundations of modern architecture, and the attack on it here

is refreshing to see. This building seems to say that of course technology is with us, but it need not be quite so revered.

Even the exposure of mechanical and electrical parts says this; or more correctly, they especially say this. The electrical tubing, the outlet boxes, and the air ducts chosen are mass-produced in thousands of shapes and sizes; they are not specialized forms like LeCorbusier's "object-types," and they are utterly devalued artistically. In the construction industry, they are akin to consumer parts; purchased in quantity, nearly disposable. We have no reverence for these forms; they give us a light feeling of shock, of restraints removed, of casualness and wit.

The architects of this small office

Karl Sliva

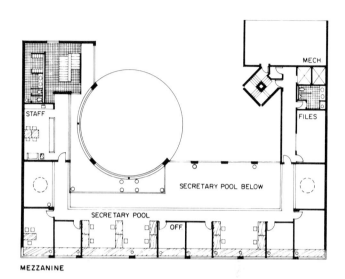

MEZZANINE

SECOND FLOOR

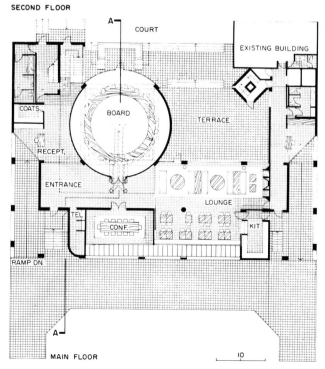

MAIN FLOOR   10

building have succeeded in expressing the human values and institutional organizational patterns which sponsored the building in the first place, as they intended to do. It is a successful building on that level, and at the same time it manages to impart new meaning to some of the inexpensive materials of our building industry.

ONTARIO MEDICAL ASSOCIATION OFFICE BUILDING, Toronto, Canada. Architects: *A. J. Diamond & Barton Myers*—Ken Viljoen, project architect; cost control: *Helyar Vermeulen, Rae, & Mauchan*; structural engineers: *M. S. Yolles & Assoc.*; mechanical engineers: *G. Granek & Assoc.*; electrical engineers: *J. Chisvin & Assoc.*; general contractor: *Richard & B. A. Ryan Limited.*

Ian Samson photos

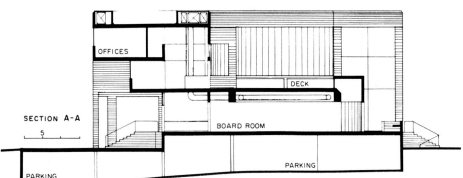

SECTION A-A

OFFICES

DECK

BOARD ROOM

PARKING

PARKING

The board room of the O.M.A. Building
(photo, above) is prominent from
any point of view around the building
and its roof has been employed as a
deck for lounging; placing a square
within a circle allows seating on
the parapet, because any seat is
usually a safe distance from the edge.

The standard spiral metal ducts in
the building, like those in the
photo at left, were cut to fit from
shop drawings in a factory, rather
than formed at the site. Each
section of duct received an inexpensive
white baked enamel finish which
could not have been applied using
site fabrication. The isometric (page
113) is the clearest representation
of the new O.M.A. building, and indicates
the architects' de-emphasis of exterior
facades; the major significance
lies in the spaces (both exterior
and interior) and with the
interior parts.

Ian Samson photos

Ian Samson photos

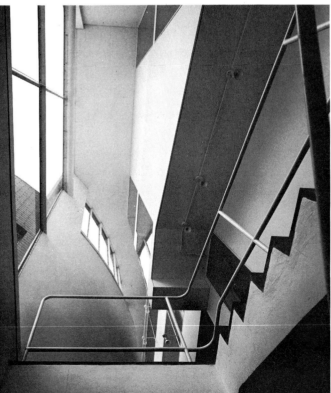

The principal stairway of the
O.M.A. Building rises from the
parking garage to the third
floor. The open doorway
of the photo above looks
through to the second floor
level, and the picture
at left was taken below the
first floor, looking straight
up. The very simple but
effective detailing of the
building is especially
evident here, along with the
absence of expensive
materials or finishes.

Corporate offices for Westinghouse
set a standard for employee amenities

The Westinghouse Corporation, through its Design Center and with the active interest of its chairman, Donald C. Burnham, has vigorously sponsored good design in both products and new facilities. The corporate office in Pittsburgh, by the Knoll Planning Unit, thus represent a standard rather than an exception, a concern for employee amenity that is common everywhere in the firm. In addition to this spirit of generosity and spaciousness, whimsey and surprise, as in this small executive conference room (below), are sprinkled throughout the building.

WESTINGHOUSE CORPORATE OFFICES, Pittsburgh, Pennsylvania. Interior designers: *Knoll Planning Unit—Lou Butler, project designer.* Client representatives *Corporate Design Center and Headquarters Works Engineering.* Art program: Eliot Noyes and Ivan Chermayeff. Consulting engineers (water-cooled light fixtures): *Meyer, Strong and Jones.*

Joseph W. Molitor photos

On the executive floor, the corner offices (acrosspage) are occupied by the presidents of the four companies that comprise the Westinghouse Corporation. Mr. Burnham's office (above) is between two of them and looks directly down the Ohio River. Each of the offices on this floor is designed to the taste of its occupant. Furnishings range from traditional mahogany pieces to the specially-designed pedestal desk at which the chairman works.

The public spaces best illustrate the pleasant spaciousness of the
building. A small grouping of comfortable furniture greets visitors
(farthest left) as they enter the otherwise forbidding lobby. The
elevator lobbies (left) and the wide corridors on each floor (below) are
also filled with planting and carefully-chosen graphics. The
reception area (right) is shared by two executive offices.

The Corporate Design Center, which has been so effective in upgrading the visual image of Westinghouse, has several open plan work spaces (below) that adapt easily to the changing projects of the center. The offices of its director, E. W. Seay (above) and assistant director, Philip Andrews (below), are exceptional examples of the personalization found in many workspaces throughout the building.

A modified office landscaping plan serves well in the work spaces of a California publisher

The small summit of Quail Hill rises over Terra Linda Valley in the Northgate section of Marin County. It is grape country, and for more than a century its vineyards have been justly famous. In 1967, an 83-acre property, which included the hilltop, was purchased by a subsidiary of the Commerce Clearing House, publishers of tax business law reports.

The owners commissioned Marquis & Stoller to masterplan the site for mixed uses and to design a small office building to occupy the crown of the hill. The structure that emerged (photo at left) is typical of the firm's approach to design. The building is fitted to the hill with obvious care. Employee parking is collected on the lower floors to leave the hillside uncluttered by cars. Offices are on the upper level, giving almost everyone a panoramic view of valley and surrounding hills (FLLW's Marin County Center stretches out just to the west).

The exteriors are formed in sand-blasted concrete and detailed in simple, crisp lines. Around the building, on the flanks of the hill, new vineyards (Cabernet Sauvignon) have been planted as an integral part of the landscaping plan. The owners anticipate a modest crop each year starting in 1972.

The interiors pivot around a landscaped three-story court that can be opened to the sky when the season permits. Court galleries, on each level, provide the building's primary internal circulation and are linked vertically by a handsomely sculpted stair (photo far right). The work areas are treated with a modified office landscape that retains corner offices but disperses its core elements. Library and conference areas are partitioned for privacy and acoustical control. Individual desks and work stations are located and positioned for maximum comfort and employee efficiency.

Inside and out, the visitor's first impression is one of quality. Closer inspection seems to confirm that impression.

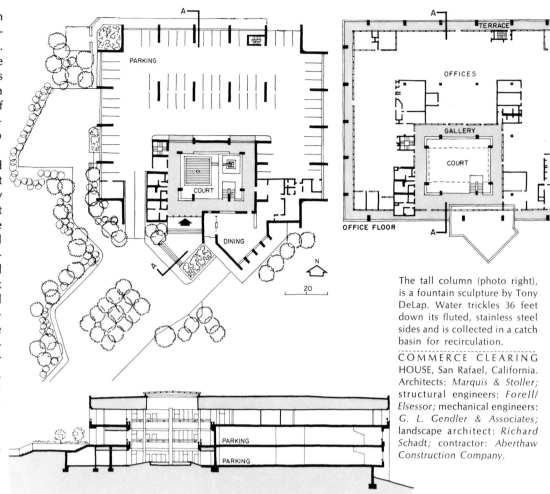

SECTION A-A

The tall column (photo right), is a fountain sculpture by Tony DeLap. Water trickles 36 feet down its fluted, stainless steel sides and is collected in a catch basin for recirculation.

COMMERCE CLEARING HOUSE, San Rafael, California. Architects: *Marquis & Stoller;* structural engineers: *Forell/ Elsessor;* mechanical engineers: *G. L. Gendler & Associates;* landscape architect: *Richard Schadt;* contractor: *Aberthaw Construction Company.*

For Squibb's World Headquarters: spaces that culminate in a compelling, skylighted gallery

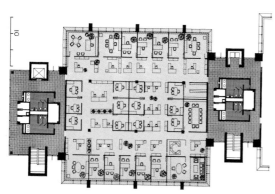

As the photographs on these pages amply reveal, the interior of this corporate headquarters for a pharmaceutical company received more than the ordinary degree of design attention. The 90 by 90 foot clusters of offices (see plan) are laid out on a regular grid but brightened with color-coded carpeting, upholstery and graphics. The dining areas include a self-service cafeteria developed with white walls, polished stainless steel fitting, and deep cylinders for lighting as well as a more intimate space with cylindrical banquettes for small groups.

At the heart of the design is a gallery (photo, across page), an enlargement of the circulation spine over the reception lobby. This spectacular multistory space is skylighted, enriched with planting and detailed in a striking pallette of handsome finish materials.

Throughout the building, the architects have established strong visual connections between inside and out.

E. R. SQUIBB & SONS, INC., Lawrenceville, New Jersey. Architects: *Hellmuth, Obata & Kassabaum, Inc.* Engineers: *LeMessurier & Associates* (structural); *J. Loring & Associates* (mechanical and electrical); contractor: *Huber & Nichols, Inc.*

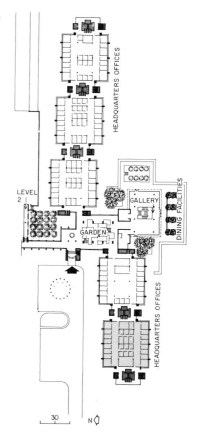

Alexander Georges photos

INTERIORS FOR SELLING

AND DISPLAY

Various interdependent forces, economic and social, have conspired in recent years to affect purchasing patterns and to radically influence the design of stores and shops. The continued development of the suburban shopping center is one. Another has been the growing economic pressure on small businesses everywhere. Linked to these two, but perhaps most important of all, has been the advent, on a large scale, of discount merchandizing. The ability of the large discount chains to buy and sell inexpensively and in large volumes has bitten deeply into the market for inexpensive goods and forced many small retailers to upgrade their merchandise, their display techniques and their images. For some, this has meant limiting the number and density of items on display, creating an "environment" for each and lighting each item in a way that enhances its visual character and accents its quality. The use of bold graphics, as in Robert Mittelstadt's design for Streeter & Quarles (page 138) or Platner's showroom for Steelcase (page 132) acts as an effective device for luring customers from the street and guiding them through the store.

Imaginative display techniques are also an important tool for selling as they arouse a customer's curiosity and intensify his desire to examine merchandise. The acrylic cylinders in Richard Acott's "Crate and Barrel" (page 136) is an excellent example. What is important, also, is that display equipment be flexible, demountable, portable and—when possible—easy to store. Shops, more than other building types, are in constant flux. Inventories often change with the season and many items have only a limited shelf life. If goods are not moving fast enough, proprietors will quickly make physical adjustments in store layout and display equipment. The lesson for architects is simple: design with flexibility in mind and do not be too enamoured of any special effects you have created. Nearly every store in this group has changed substantially since these photographs were taken. That is not the symptom of a store designer's failure. It is the badge of his success.

Laminated wood "flowers" give a bland space drama and spatial modulation

In a space previously occupied by a French restaurant in La Maison Francaise at Rockefeller Center, Victor Lundy has created an extremely effective and intriguing two-level showroom for the Singer Company. Continuing his interest in creating very architectural interiors by the use of laminated wood forms, he has unified and dramatized the big space here with a series of wood "flowers" which create a series of bays and vistas, all reflected and extended by mirrored walls. Neutral beige tones dominate the scheme as a foil for the brilliant colors of the fabric displays. With the exception of the chairs, Lundy designed all the interior furnishings, such as tables, display tables of glass and wood, and counters. Grasscloth covers walls not mirrored, and the entire space is carpeted. Chairs and stools are upholstered in linen velour. The lighting throughout was carefully planned for the dual function of highlighting displays and emphasizing the dramatic shapes of the "flowers." An open well and escalators are used to interconnect the two levels. Rockefeller Center, Inc. acted as contractor; engineering consultants were Jaros, Baum & Bolles (mechanical) and Edwards & Hjorth (structural).

George Cserna photos

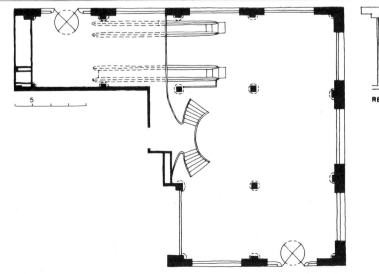

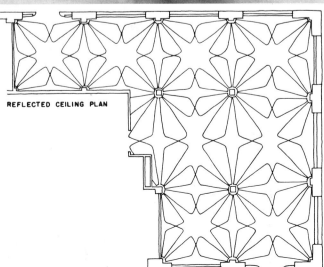

REFLECTED CEILING PLAN

5

Images of light and motion for the Steelcase showroom at Chicago's Merchandise Mart

THE PRECISE LINE OF THE PRODUCTS IS ECHOED in the precision of the over-all showroom design. All the lights and electrical work are neatly placed above the horizontal glass panels and fixed to the ceiling. Spaces above, as well as below, the glass are airconditioned to reduce the heat load. The glass itself is considerably thinner (quarter-inch) than normally used in this country, reducing costs and weight. The panels rest on simple rotating clips suspended on a standard metal strut system; the corners of the glass were cut out where needed for sprinklers.

All the display devices are demountable and portable; there is a storeroom to one side of the main display area for those items not in current use. The glass display islands may be walked on.

A smooth transition is made between the "glassiness" of the exhibition space (the back portion of which is shown here) and the more compact, efficient work and conference rooms beyond, by creating an open alcove with a dropped plaster ceiling and backed by a brightly-lighted wall of warm-toned leather. Sympathetic colors (browns, beiges, yellows, orange) are used for upholstery and accent colors in the office areas. Corridors to either side are lined with displays of files and cabinets to further help the transition from purely exhibit to functional areas.

Explaining why—except in the real, working offices—there has been no attempt to create "office settings" in the showroom, Warren Platner comments that "it was our intent to create an exhibition space where the products shown are seen for what they are—objects of quality and utility—not to be confused with arbitrary decisions as to what one designer might think an office should look like. In other words, we put the products in the context of a showcase (and hence 'exhibition space' is a much better description than 'showroom' which conjures visions of model rooms with their confusing image of what to do with a product). We wanted a very light space, a luminous one, so you could see everything clearly—and of course the reflecting glass furthers that too."

The very simplicity of the project (which, characteristically, was achieved only by a long and painstaking design process) gives it an extraordinarily strong and fresh sophistication that should make it a high point in the Mart.

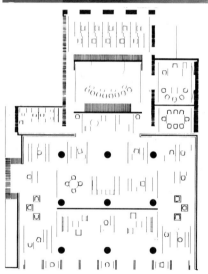

SHIMMERING, SUBTLE REFLECTIONS EXTEND THE REAL SPACE and add considerable glamor and effectiveness to the Steelcase products displayed in the new exhibit in Chicago's Merchandise Mart.

Warren Platner has created a real traffic-stopper in the big, busy showroom center by minimizing the usual "room setting" techniques and creating a deceptively simple, reflecting space which enhances both the furniture on exhibit and the visiting customers. Almost all surfaces in the basically loft-like space were coated white—vinyl floors, painted plaster walls and structural ceilings. A sparkling glass shell has been created within this room for the major display and exhibit area. Countless glass doors line the corridor facade and the walls; all doors are operable (and placed a few inches out from the walls) to assure easy cleaning and maximum sparkle, and to permit a changing series of graphics behind.

Horizontal glass panels are suspended below the ceiling, which is fitted with an adjustable track system of spot and floodlights; within the room, islands and cases of glass delineate display groupings. The end effect is an eye-catching glitter which dematerializes the confining spaces, provides an endless series of subtle reflections of everything in the room. Color and accent are provided by the furniture displayed, by the sparingly used graphics, and by people walking through. All the graphics are changeable, and intended to be changed. In this initial installation, the translucent images on the side walls are all x-rays of Steelcase construction details, and the big black and white mural represents body motion and implications for posture and comfort. The hatched areas shown on the plan at left are floor-to-ceiling walls of the company's line of files and cabinets, handsomely arranged into Mondrian-like compositions. Thus, apart from a very few leather paneled walls toward the back, all wall surfaces are products or their reflections.

STEELCASE SHOWROOM, Chicago, Illinois. Architects: *Warren Platner—project associates, Mark Morgaridge, Robert Brauer, Paul Sargent, Lawrence Kilbourn, Lee Ahlstrom;* mechanical engineer: *John L. Altieri;* graphics: *Vance Jonson and Joel Margulies, Unimark International;* contractor: *E. H. Marhoefer, Jr. Co.*

At Crate & Barrel,

Crate & Barrel is a retail chain that specializes in well-designed imported housewares and colorful Scandinavian fabrics. For its outlet in Oakbrook, Illinois, architect Richard Acott designed a restrained but richly-textured background for the display of merchandise with high visual impact. Quarry tile, clinker brick and rough-sawn beech cubes contrast strongly with crystal stemware and high-glaze china. Lighting is generally subdued and used to dramatize individual displays. Bright-colored umbrellas provide an overhead accent and give the space added height.

Despite the profusion of colors and shapes, the texture contrasts, and the variety of display techniques, the store retains an appealing clarity and a relaxed sense of order.

CRATE & BARREL, Oakbrook, Illinois. Owner: *Euromarket Design, Inc.* Architects: *Richard Acott & Associates;* mechanical engineers: *Khatib-Vandiver & Associates;* contractor: *Sinclair Construction Co.*

Hedrich-Blessing photos

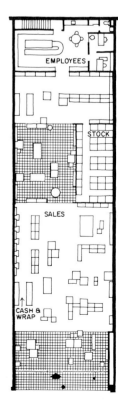

a neutral background lets the products speak for themselves

Streeter & Quarles West: powerful supergraphics are used to attract potential

shoppers from the street

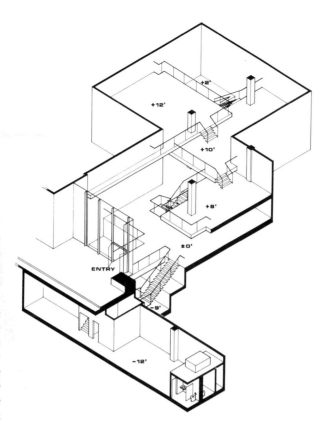

Joshua Freiwald

Robert Mittelstadt's design for Streeter and Quarles West, a San Francisco sporting goods shop also placed in an old building, is based on maximum transparency. The brilliantly-lit interior with its colorful merchandise is separated from the street by the least-substantial glass wall possible. The enormous lettering on the window and on the transparent beam in front of it, the banner and the colors all draw attention to the store without diluting the openness of the design. Furthermore, the transparency of the new store, surrounded by a solid framework of classical architecture, provides a bold contrast with the other stores. Boldness, long understood as an effective visual selling tool by roadside retailers, is the newest design technique in presenting high-quality merchandise. It does not always work. But when bold color and graphics are coupled with thoroughly disciplined functional and spatial concepts, the result can be a compelling magnet for those who respond to an exciting, up-to-the-minute setting for merchandizing. The giant photo-murals of sportsmen in action and vivid colors inside Streeter and Quarles West are used to draw people in. Then they guide them through a series of well planned inter-relating floor planes which might be confusing without such large-scale reference elements. The over-all effect, once inside the store, is quite restrained. But no matter, by then the brilliant colors of the sports equipment and clothing take over to attract the buyer's eye.

A large but awkwardly-shaped volume (in what was once a major downtown San Francisco department store, now divided into several elegant shops and a parking garage), was the envelope with which Robert Mittelstadt had to work designing Streeter & Quarles West. The drawing, see above indicating a total of 24 feet between the lowest and highest levels, also shows how he developed "a series of 'floating' platforms that serve two functions: to provide a labyrinthine attraction for customers and to maximize the sales area." As the photograph on this page shows, the easy flow of the floor levels, one to another, could have a truly magnetic quality for the shopper. Beyond that, he has developed a series of flexible furnishings and fixtures to complement the spatial scheme. As the business grows, he finds himself still involved: tuning the lighting system, designing new fixtures and working with the sales staff on display set-up. But the basic conceptual

Joshua Freiwald

framework of the shop, which grew out of careful study of the existing space by the architect, has proved to be the most flexible aspect of the design.

STREETER & QUARLES WEST San Francisco. Owner: *Michael Harrington, Inc.*; architects: *Robert Mittelstadt, Architect and Monte S. Bell*—project design: *Robert Mittelstadt*; structural engineers: *Forell-Chan*; electrical engineer: *Mel Camissa*; photo murals: *Lloyd Johnson*.

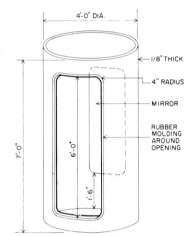

4'-0" DIA.

1/8" THICK

4" RADIUS

MIRROR

RUBBER MOLDING AROUND OPENING

7'-0"

6'-0"

1'-6"

Jeremiah Bragstadt

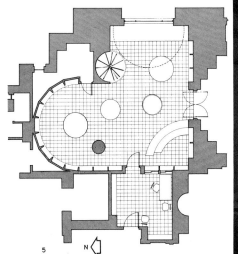

Up-to-date book-store fitted skillfully into the elegant forms of the past

The program called upon archi-tects Robinson & Mills to de-sign a small, modern bookstore off the grand, neo-classic en-trance lobby of San Francisco's Museum of Art. Because of the building's landmark character, no external sign was allowed. Identifying graphics were re-stricted to the overhead, inte-rior curved surface facing the street window. The architects began with a space that had functioned as two adjacent stor-age rooms. The central column was simply a fact of life. To set up a gentle flow pattern, using the intruding column as a pivot, a curved wall was in-troduced for book display. The circular theme is continued in the print rack, the sales desk and the portable, plastic-domed display cabinets. To emphasize this easy, uninterrupted flow visually, the designers striped the top of the walls and col-umns in black and white—a feature that is playfully reflected on the ceiling of silver vinyl. Other finish materials are kept light in color to augment and enliven these colorful, overhead reflections.

MUSEUM BOOKSTORE, San Francisco Museum of Art. Architects: *Robinson & Mills (Jeffrey L. Teel, project de-signer)*; mechanical engineer: *Paul E. Rosenthal*; electrical engineers: *Darm-sted-Parenti & Associates*; graphic consultants: *Reis & Manwaring*; con-tractor: *Jacks & Irvine, Inc.*

5   N

Morley Baer photos

A powerful heavy timber enclosure unifies a potpourri of shops and products

Otto Baitz photos

Is this the shopping center of the future? The first shopping centers, twenty-five years ago, were a strip of stores along the highway. Next another strip of stores was placed across a mall. Then, the last word it seemed, a roof was added. Now, what if you threw out all the plastic shrubbery and filled those empty malls with small shops so close together that you'd have to walk through one to get to the next? Voila! That's Heritage Village Bazaar.

In his latest project for the retirement community in Southbury, Connecticut, Warren Callister has combined the ancient concept of the bazaar with a 19th century system of construction, heavy timber. The result is definitely up-to-date, in effect, the Miesian "Universal Space" enriched with vibrant color, form and activity.

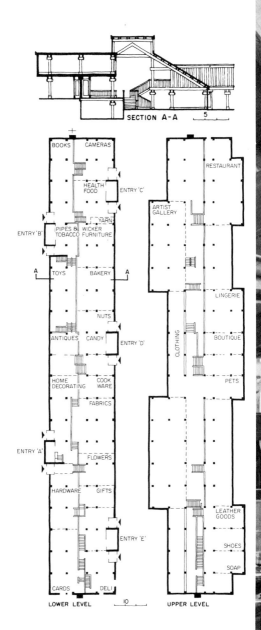

SECTION A-A   5

LOWER LEVEL

BOOKS | CAMERAS
HEALTH FOOD | ENTRY 'C'
PIPES & TOBACCO | WICKER FURNITURE
ENTRY 'B' | YARN
A | TOYS | BAKERY | A
NUTS
ANTIQUES | CANDY | ENTRY 'D'
HOME DECORATING | COOK WARE
FABRICS
ENTRY 'A' | FLOWERS
HARDWARE | GIFTS
ENTRY 'E'
CARDS | DELI

UPPER LEVEL   10

RESTAURANT
ARTIST GALLERY
LINGERIE
CLOTHING | BOUTIQUE
PETS
LEATHER GOODS
SHOES
SOAP

In addition to two half levels at grade, mezzanines in each projecting bay provide lively spatial interplay in the 420-foot long building. The four different levels are joined across the tall central spine (clerestory faces east) by frequent stairways, above.

Since Heritage Village Bazaar opened last August, more than twenty small businesses selected by the Paparazzo Development Corporation staff have set up on the various levels of the building. Five boldly-lettered cubes hang in the space, and divide it into sections. Frequent maps key the various shops to the appropriate section. One of the most elusive charms of the building is the pleasant sense of confusion, of being overwhelmed with choice of things to see, samples to nibble, and crannies to explore.

Some of the shops, like the Nut Kettle with its orange roasting chimney, left, have modulated the entire space although most have fitted into the space with a minimum of additional construction. The most outstanding exception is the Carousel toy shop right, (p. 142) by New Haven architect Caswell Cooke. Built of 150 brightly-painted 2x2 frame modules (18 by 36 by 54 inches) bolted together, the shop has an internal walkway which takes grandparents and others on a lengthy tour of the available gifts. At times the walkway rises twelve feet above the floor on which it is built. Conceived entirely in model form, the store was built within the Bazaar a module at a time. Except for a few specially reinforced sections such as the main stairway, the stacked modules support their own weight. A film was made of the one-day erection process including the reactions of several children turned loose on the newly-built structure. Perhaps the best test of the flexibility of Callister's building is that another architect has been able to provide such an appropriate counterpoint within the framework.

The exterior of the Bazaar, designed in the now-familiar esthetic of the rest of Heritage Village, combines solidness and good scale with careful siting.

- -

THE BAZAAR AT THE VILLAGE GREEN, Heritage Village, Southbury, Connecticut. Owner: *Paparazzo Development Corporation.* Architects: *Callister and Payne;* associated architects: *August Rath;* structural engineer: *Glenn R. Nelson;* graphics consultant: *Barbara Stauffacher;* contractor: *Paparazzo Development Corp.*

The virile heavy timber construction of the Bazaar is especially evident at those places where the roof begins at the first floor eave and continues right up to the clerestory, above. Here, in the wicker furniture shop adjacent to the toy store, light bounces off the sloping ceiling from fixtures boxed into the beams bracing the central columns. Rising 32 feet, these columns, three 3x12's and two 2x12's bolted together, evoke memories of the past for Heritage Villagers while providing solid support. The lateral bracing is accented by 6x14 bolsters.

**Four large
chain stores
anchor the corners
of a huge
shopping mall
in Southern
California**

The Eastridge Regional Mall in San Jose, California, is one of the largest shopping developments in the country—1,750,000 square feet of retail area—and just as any mall with two levels was revolutionary six years ago, so Eastridge's three levels of shopping in the central court (photo, below right) is considered unusual today. Neither the architect, Avner Naggar, nor the principal developer and builder, Alfred Taubman of The Taubman Company justifies a three-level court in visual terms, or as just the newest way to create an exciting space. According to these men, there are very real economic pressures, and pressures inherent in the nature of people themselves, that are generating three-level malls today, and these pressures will continue to make shopping malls more and more compact. That seems to be the key word—compactness—which of course sets no limit on total size. Taubman believes there *is* a limit to the amount of walking a shopper will willingly do, however, which sets limits on how far from each other the large "magnet" department stores may be. Also small retailers do not want to be too far from the action around the central court of any shopping center. Further, if there is a limit to the amount of walking any shopper is cheerfully willing to do, that limit seems to be extended a little if the shopper's goal—the store he or she is trying to reach—can actually be seen. That is, there are advantages to people being able to quickly comprehend how big a place is.

All of these issues lead inevitably to designs that compress and concentrate activities, such as the three levels at Eastridge.

SITE PLAN

Actually, the mall is more complicated than that, with four different levels inside that we may call 0 ft, + 6 ft, + 18 ft and + 24 ft. The west end of the mall near Penney's (see section and plans, following page) is divided into the normal two levels (0 ft, + 18 ft) and the east end near Sears has two different levels (6 ft and 24 ft). Where these two malls meet at the central court an intermediate gallery at + 12 ft is created, thus making the three level (0, + 12 ft, + 24 ft) major space. One level should not be thought of as secondary to any

other, and this was accomplished at Eastridge by sloping the parking lots up or down. The site (plan, below left) has been sectioned into quadrants, with the ring road that circles all the parking areas established at one constant elevation. Each quadrant of parking meets the building at different elevations, so that each level inside has direct access to parking at the same level. This required substantial land grading, but most of the existing mature trees on the site were saved through use of retaining walls or tree wells.

The exteriors of the mall

(photos, below left) utilize face brick, poured-in-place concrete and pre-cast concrete. The angularity of these facades echo one of the major themes inside that makes the Eastridge Mall visually cohesive; that is, the common slope of the walls, step risers, and ceiling skylights as shown in the interior below. What appears to be multiple angles in the storefronts and fascias is in fact only one angle, with a three-to-seven slope, chosen because it fits exactly within the structural grid of 24-foot by 28-foot column bays. The terrazzo tiling of the floor,

the edges of the many pools and fountains, the stair risers, and the edges of the intricately skylit ceiling all repeat this angle to establish a sense of fluid spaciousness in the center.

The Eastridge Mall draws on a residential population of about 500,000 people, and is the only large suburban commercial center in its area. Consequently, the developers have concrete plans to establish an office complex and low-rise residential units in second and third phases. They own property west and north of Quimby Road, adjacent to the mall, and

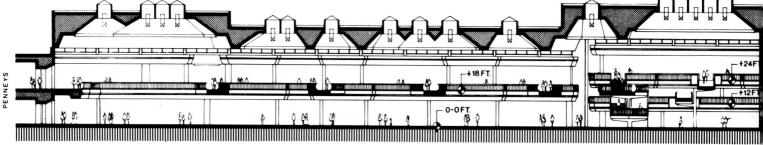

LONGITUDINAL SECTION

PENNEYS

+24 FT
+18 FT.
+12 FT
0-0 FT.

design is underway on these additional projects. Alfred Taubman estimates that about 300 new apartments have already been generated in the immediate neighborhood of the mall, that would never have been built otherwise. A major mall such as Eastridge may generate 5,000 new jobs in a community, with a complementary need for new housing, according to Taubman.

The ice arena near Liberty House, (see plans, below) and the Community Hall near Penney's are both subsidized by the center as public spaces: Both can be reached directly from outside, when the rest of the center is closed.

The plastic dome of the information booth (large photo left) dominates one end of the pool, cascading gently downhill within the space, and there are rather luxurious carpeted seating areas at four different locations on the main floor. The plans below indicate the many changes in level within the mall, particularly in the major long arcade leading to the Sears store (see photo opposite). Each change in level uses only three risers to eliminate the need for close handrailing, and of course there are ramps throughout for wheelchairs or carts. The many bridges are apparent in the lower plan, so shoppers may easily reach any store on an opposite gallery.

The lighting at Eastridge is based on a different original premise than the lighting for most large shopping malls. Rather than allow the fixture to disappear in the background, thereby revealing only the object being lit, the lighting consultants here preferred that fixtures be revealed as objects. Evans and Hillmann make the point that any viewer becomes more involved in the lighting of the space, and understands it better, if he can see the fixtures that produce the light. This point-of-view requires that prominent fixtures be closely integrated with the architectural forms, and this has certainly been accomplished at Eastridge. The mall is skylit, but within each bay of skylighting have been placed special lighting fixtures used at night or cloudy days, so that the light, whether bright sun or evening, always come from generally the same

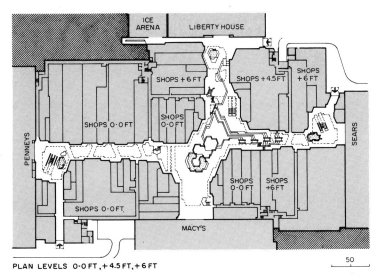

PLAN LEVELS 0·0 FT, +4.5 FT, +6 FT   50

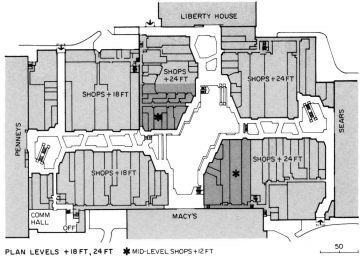

PLAN LEVELS +18 FT, 24 FT ✱ MID-LEVEL SHOPS +12 FT   50

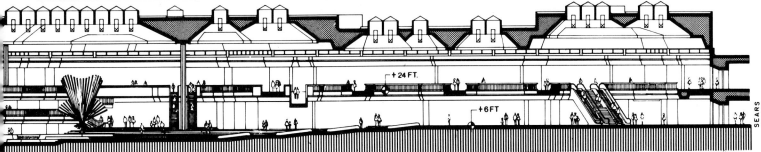

25

area of the ceiling (see below).

The fixtures themselves that Evans and Hillmann designed are worth noting, and one is shown in detail in the photo below. The basic components are a standard highbay industrial luminaire with a 50 per cent louver for brightness control, pairs of 400-watt mercury lamps and panels of acrylic plastic, intersecting at 45 degrees. The luminaire is wrapped in a rectangular housing painted white, and a rectangular clear acrylic basket, containing the intersecting panels of acrylic, is suspended beneath the luminaire as shown in the photo.

The fixture lights the floor and ceiling planes simultaneously. All light rays striking the intersecting planes of acrylic at 42 degrees or greater are reflected up and out onto the ceiling panels. The remaining light rays are passing through these panels to provide lighting at the floor. The result is a general glow of light in the whole mall space, as the photographs indicated, aided by the more normal cove incandescent lighting at the gallery soffits. It is an almost shadowless environment when compared to the strong lights and shadows of the Columbia system. The specially designed pink and blue filters at the bottom of the acrylic shroud are there to alter the vertical light rays, according to Evans and Hillmann, creating subtle color nuances at the floor level, along with high illumination. The reflected ceiling plan (below) shows the complex pattern of skylights and light sources within the mall. In one of the mall cafeterias, clear-glass globes hang from the ceiling like bunches of grapes, acting as reflectors for the light source above them.

EASTRIDGE REGIONAL SHOPPING MALL, San Jose, California. Architect: *Avner Naggar.* Owners: *Bayshore Properties and Homart Development Co.* Structural engineers: *Butzbach, Bar-Din & Dagan;* soils engineers: *Woodward, Lundgren & Associates;* mechanical engineers: *Yoshpe Engineers;* electrical engineers: *Edward S. Shinn & Associates;* lighting consultants: *Evans & Hillmann,* landscape architects: *Lawrence Halprin & Associates;* traffic engineers: *Barton-Aschman Associates;* general contractor: *The Taubman Company, Inc.*

SECTION @ CENTRAL COURT

ELEV. +4.5 FT.

MALL REFLECTED CEILING PLAN

N

A showroom reached only by elevator

When stores or shops or, in this case, wholesale showrooms are buried deep within a building—and therefore usually accessible only to people who know they are there—it becomes more important than ever to make them distinctive and therefore worth a visit. This showroom is for Charlie's Girls, an apparel manufacturer which is a division of a single larger company. Here bold graphics have been introduced to attract the eyes of prospective buyers and to compete effectively with the other companies located in adjacent spaces on the same floor of the office building. In Charlie's Girls, an undulating wall—with the name of the company written both large and small on it—separates the waiting and office spaces (right and immediately below) from the actual selling areas (below right). For the greater part of its length the wall is formed by cabinetwork which houses the showroom's line of ladies' sports clothes, and these cabinets are lit from within by concealed lights. Along the window wall there are individual selling booths defined by free-standing panels with bars for hanging clothes (right). These panels can, when necessary, be moved aside for seasonal fashion shows to allow room for spectators and the processions of the models.

SHOWROOMS FOR CHARLIE'S GIRLS, New York City. Architects: *Robert A. M. Stern and John S. Hagmann.* Consultant: *Don Wise Advertising & Company* (graphics). Custom cabinetwork: *William Somerville & Company.* General contractor: *Chanin Construction Corporation.*

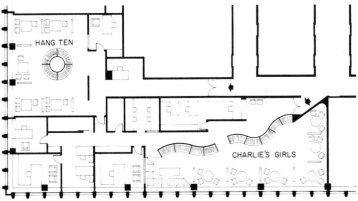

INTERIORS FOR DINING

AND DRINKING

The architect designing restaurants, cafes and bars has just the same problems he has always had—to plan efficient spaces for the storage and preparation of food, clear avenues of circulation for food service and, in the public spaces, a visual theme or atmosphere that gives the dining areas a clear identity. What has changed is that his job is harder now since the restaurant business has suffered through difficult times in recent years, and the prospects for the immediate future, say many restauranteurs, are little improved. Many of the problems seem to be chronic: inflation, high turnover of personnel, a capricious public, limited hours and a highly competitive business. The restaurants that have suffered most have been elegant establishments with long menus, soft seats and expense account prices. Those that have fared best, temporarily at least, are the "trendy" places where an "in" crowd have suddenly found it fashionable to dine or drink. Why a restaurant that has struggled to survive for years suddenly finds its tables full of beautiful people every night, all night, is as bewildering to restauranteurs as it is to anyone.

The restaurants and bars included in this section cater to a wide variety of customers and a range of public taste. The dining room at Squibb's World Headquarters by Hellmuth, Obata & Kassabaum (page 164) and John Fowler's renovation of the Yale Freshman Commons (page 158) are as different as two dining spaces can be. One is soothing and restrained; the other glittering and wildly animated. Both are successful. In Warren Platner's design for "Le Monde," (page 156) fine food and drink are not only the consumables but also the visual theme. The other examples we have included are successful interiors for a variety of different reasons. What each has in common is the use of a very few architectural elements, few finish materials and little wasted design motion, subdued but flattering lighting, acoustical control and most important of all perhaps, an aura of elegance that lingers as a potent afterimage long after the Beef Wellington or the Tuborg have been forgotten.

Robert C. Lautman photos

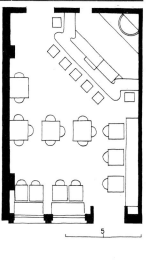

Beautiful detailing in white oak and mirror glass give this Georgetown bar an aura of quiet refinement

Space-expanding techniques with mirrors and beautiful craftsmanship give a sense of unusual ease and quality to this addition by Hugh Jacobsen to Clydes Bar in Georgetown. All woods are a lustrous, clear white oak: oak strips for the hung ceiling covering the air-conditioning ducts; lacquered oak flooring for the walls; an oak laminate for banquettes, tables and bar. To contrast with all this wood, all floors are surfaced with a white, unglazed ceramic tile. The chairs are also oak and covered with black plastic. The comfortable bar stools were fabricated from brass-plated tractor seats; this metal is echoed in a mirror-finished brass gutter to the bar, and in all hardware. Great spaciousness and sparkle are added to this monochromatic scheme by extremely effective lighting and a knowing use of mirrors. To visually extend the height of the walls, mirror was laminated to the existing ceiling around the perimeter of the room; the bar and banquettes are visually extended by floor-to-ceiling mirror strips. With the careful, handsome detailing and execution of everything in the bar, Jacobsen has clearly met his design objectives: "Clydes Bar opened in 1966 with dark-stained, beaded-siding walls of pine, bentwood chairs, Tiffany lamps and low camp. It was a howling success. I was retained to add more room in the building next door. Under the premise that any camp is too much, my objective was to use traditional materials in a new way, but to keep the pub saloon-like atmosphere that had proved so successful." The contractor for the project was Edwin Davis.

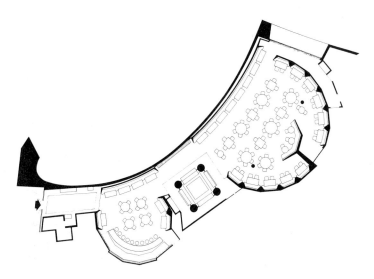

Alexandre Georges photos

Warren Platner's design for Le Monde Restaurant adds new elegance to TWA's terminal at New York's Kennedy airport

Fine food and drink are the things here and the visual character is made of these elements, their preparation, and the furnishings and fittings necessary to properly enjoy them.

The vocabulary of materials is simple: clear glass and mirrors, polished stainless steel, natural leather, and myriad custom-designed lighting fixtures set in a plaster ceiling. Carpets are dark red. Deeply-absorbing wool tapestries, designed by the architect in collaboration with Sheila Hicks, flank the back bar (photo, right). The space and its forms flow together into near fantasy compounded of softly fractured images and reflected detail (photo, preceding page). TWA wanted a warm, rich, intimate ambiance for dining and drinking. They got it with little more than the necessary functional elements splendidly conceived and elegantly detailed. Mechanical engineers: *Jaros, Baum & Bolles;* contractor: *Hennigan Construction Co.*

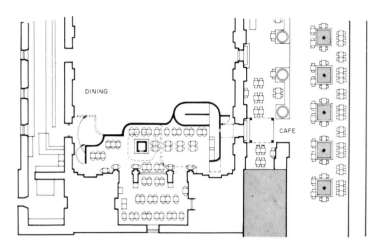

Norman McGrath photos

Remodelled space in Yale Commons gives the undergraduates a spectacular cafe

Working with a rigid program in a monumental, turn-of-the-century space, John Fowler has created a spectacular cafe for Yale University undergraduates.

The facility has to operate without interrupting the normal ceremonial functions of the Commons itself, and has to be able to return its floor space to the Commons for large banquets at least six times a year. The architect met these requirements by designing a combination folding and hinged partition, mounted on casters and anchored to an enclosed stair. When thrown open, the cafe is part of the larger space. When closed, as shown, the space becomes a private, shimmering world of mixed texture and blurred form. Sheets of specular aluminum, mounted on the curved partition, contrast brightly with the magnificent but somber oak carvings and reflect them in distorted and sometimes frenzied detail. Red and purple banners, hung overhead, filter the light and add the right dose of brilliant color. Structural engineer: *Associated Engineering, Herman Spiegel;* contractor: *George B. Macomber Co.*

For Boston sports fans, a place to relax and talk about the game

Two problems faced architects Keith Kroeger and Leonard Perfido when they were commissioned to redesign the Boston Madison Square Garden Club at the Boston Garden Arena. First, they had to solve the functional problems involved in more than doubling the size of the original club into space .formerly occupied by Arena offices and a concessions commissary. Secondly, and more important, they had to retain the flavor of the club, a gathering place for members attending events at the Boston Arena for more than forty years. Materials and furnishings were chosen carefully. The ash boards and chair frames are lightly stained to accent the grain. The chairs, banquettes and the bar arm rest are upholstered in stretch vinyl. Natural linen covers the wall panels and green wool carpeting continues up the front of the bar, (right). Engineers: *LeMessurier and Associates,* structural; *Reardon and Turner,* mechanical; contractor: *Turner Construction Co.*

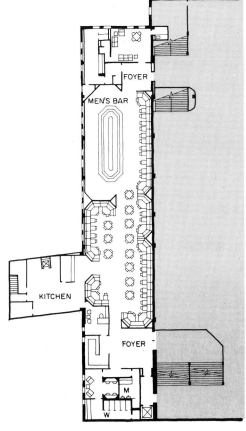

Dining space for a midwestern motor inn changes its mood at different times during the day

The owners of this Kansas City motor inn commissioned the Urban Architects to renovate the inn's main dining and entertaining areas. The first challenge was to accomplish the renovation with as little interruption to normal hotel service as possible. Second, and more difficult, the architects had to plan the space so that it could be bright and cheerful in the morning when it serves as a coffee shop and more relaxed and intimate in the evening for quiet dining. The architects attacked this problem directly and simply. They selected reflective finish surfaces and then provided variable lighting levels carefully keyed to these surfaces. By adjusting the lighting levels, finish surfaces—as well as dinner- and glass-ware—either sparkle or become subdued. Mirrors, mounted on the side walls over the booths, contribute to this process and also serve to extend the space visually.

Colors are generally dark and restrained: rich brown leather for seating, brown and black for carpeting, black laminate on table tops. The generous application of light wood trim, occasional panels of red felt and a warm reflective character keep this elegant space from ever becoming overly somber.

DOWNTOWNER MOTOR INN, Kansas City, Missouri, owner: *Downtowner Corporation*. Architects: *Urban Architects (Stephen Abend, partner-in-charge)*; mechanical engineers: *Smith & Boucher*; contractor: *Jenkins & Blaine Construction Company*.

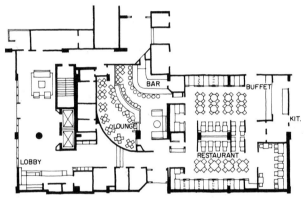

Paul Kivett photos

Alexandre Georges

Strong but elegant details for the corporate dining space at Squibb's world headquarters

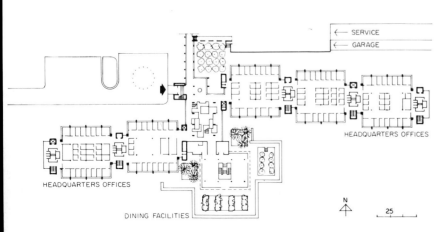

SERVICE
GARAGE

HEADQUARTERS OFFICES

HEADQUARTERS OFFICES

DINING FACILITIES

N

25

The corporate dining spaces at the Squibb World Headquarters Building in Lawrenceville, New Jersey show much more than the ordinary concern for employee amenity. Designed by Hellmuth-Obata & Kassabaum, these spaces also betray more than the ordinary design attention. The structural framing is poured-in-place concrete sprayed with a textured finish for warmth and sound absorption. Various seating arrangements including cylindrical banquettes offer diners desireable options. Downlighting is all incandescent.

E. R. SQUIBB & SONS, INC. Lawrenceville, New Jersey. Architects: *Hellmuth-Obata & Kassabaum, Inc.* Engineers: *Le Messurier & Associates* (structural); *Joseph R. Loring & Associates* (mechanical/electrical). Food service: *Flambert & Flambert, Inc.*, Contractor: *Huber, Hunt & Nichols.*

INTERIORS FOR THE

PERFORMING ARTS

The performing arts have always faced an economic struggle in this country but during the mid '60s, their common plight improved as a result both of Federal and State subsidy as well as the generosity of many patrons and private benefactors. New cultural facilities sprang up in cities, large and small, and on many a university campus. The hotly debated issue was whether a single house could be designed to accommodate musical events, drama and dance equally well or whether the ideal requirements for each were incompatible and could only be satisfied by separate facilities designed to the precise requirements of each. Could an opera house with its heroic themes, productions and massed vocal forces host a string quartet or soloist without overwhelming him? Nobody really knew. Some cities tried producing houses with areas of seating that could be physically closed off and ceilings of "acoustical clouds" that could be lowered and realigned. But elsewhere as at Lincoln Center's Juilliard School of Music (page 168) or at University of Illinois' Krannert Center (page 178) a variety of special halls were clustered to create arts complexes.

During this same period, the ground rules for drama production were expanding. Actors and directors though still working on proscenium stages were experimenting more actively than ever with thrust stages, arena seating and theater in the round. New theaters, like Cincinnati's Playhouse in the Park (page 190) by Hardy Holzman Pfeiffer Associates required flexible stage capabilities and the message of experiment was carried into every part of the house. The same architects remodelled an old carriage house into the Newark Community Center of the Arts (page 192), a small scale but appealing rehearsal and performance space for neighborhood youngsters.

The section closes with two film theaters, not spaces for the performing arts technically, but exceptionally handsome houses with many of the same design problems. Like the others, the designers of these two film theaters solved the functional problems of comfort, acoustics and sightlines as well as the problem of visual coherence with more than the ordinary design skill.

For an urban site: a school of music fitted together with a sorcerer's skill

Contained within the serene, well-ordered, simple and rather innocent facades of the new Juillard School (the world's first conservatory for all the performing arts) is an almost infinite variety of spaces fitted together with a sorcerer's skill in an arrangement as intricate as a Chinese puzzle. In the process of developing the kind of spatial organization required to satisfy the complex Juilliard program in a tight urban site with severe height limitations, Pietro Belluschi and his associate architects Eduardo Catalano and Helge Westermann have managed to tuck and fit the assorted instructional and performance facilities of a good-sized campus into one integrated structure.

Solving the structural, mechanical, acoustical and theater engineering problems posed by the organization of elements in this building called for all the skill and ingenuity at the command of the architects and their consultants. Rooms which on a larger site would normally be widely separated for acoustical reasons are stacked above each other, overlap or nestle side by side. The column-free larger halls which in most performing arts complexes are composed as separate elements under their own long-span roofs, are here framed to carry eccentric loads from the complicated spaces on the floors above. Minimum clearances due to the height restrictions made the coordination of structural elements, mechanical ductwork and stage equipment a challenging problem.

In the 12-year struggle to get Juilliard designed and built, the architects, with great patience and willingness to start over, produced about 70 different sets of preliminary drawings. The architects and engineers produced over 300 on-the-job sketches to coordinate structure and equipment during the construction process.

Because Juilliard remained in the design stage for so long and was begun last, its designers learned from the mistakes made in the other buildings at Lincoln Center. There was time, also, to sensitively adapt the school to its surroundings as it gradually became evident what its surroundings would be. Juilliard's travertine-sheathed exterior, a gift of the Italian government, is sympathetically related to the handsome facades of the Vivian Beaumont Theater by Saarinen with which it shares a small plaza to the north of the main square.

Juilliard's interiors are in some ways better than those of the other buildings. Its beautifully shaped wood panelled auditoriums, for example, prove that it is possible to create elegant halls in contemporary terms without resorting to skimpy evocations of the gilt, plaster and crystal decor of the great halls of the past.

The art with which the arts are housed affects them profoundly for the better. It is fortunate, therefore, that the incredible effort on the part of Belluschi and his team has produced such a fine building. Since Juilliard is a school for the musicians, actors and dancers of the future, it is appropriate that the best building at Lincoln Center should be theirs.

THE JUILLIARD SCHOOL, New York, N.Y. Owner: *Lincoln Center for the Performing Arts, Inc.;* constituent institution: *The Juilliard School.* Architect: *Pietro Belluschi—Eduardo Catalano and Helge Westermann,* associated architects; *Frederick Taylor, Robert Brannen and Joseph V. Morog,* project architects; *Austris J. Vitols, Robert P. Burns and William E. Pederson,* designers; *Joseph Zelazny,* resident architect and engineer. Structural engineer: *Paul Weidlinger;* mechanical and electrical engineers: *Jaros, Baum and Bolles;* stage design consultant: *Jean Rosenthal Associates, Inc.;* acoustical consultant: *Heinrich Keilholz;* special structures engineer: *Olaf Soot;* organ consultant: *Walter Holtkamp;* interior furnishings: *Helge Westermann;* contractor: *Walsh Construction Company.*

Model: Lincoln Center for the Performing Arts

As the sections indicate, the Juilliard School has three general zones from the sub-basement to the penthouse. Beginning four stories below the street, the lowest zone includes the performance areas of the Juilliard Theater and Alice Tully Hall, their supporting facilities, and a portion of the mechanical equipment. The uppermost zone, below the mechanical penthouse, consists of three instructional floors.

This intermediate zone contains the public areas, administrative services, lounges, Paul Recital Hall and the Drama Workshop.

A. Juilliard Theater
B. Drama Workshop
C. Lila Acheson Wallace Library
D. Orchestra rehearsal and recording studio
E. Paul Recital Hall
F. Alice Tully Hall

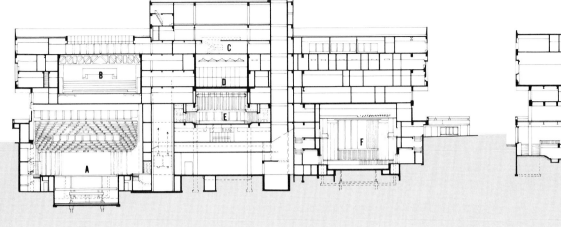
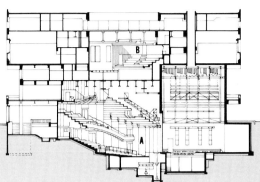

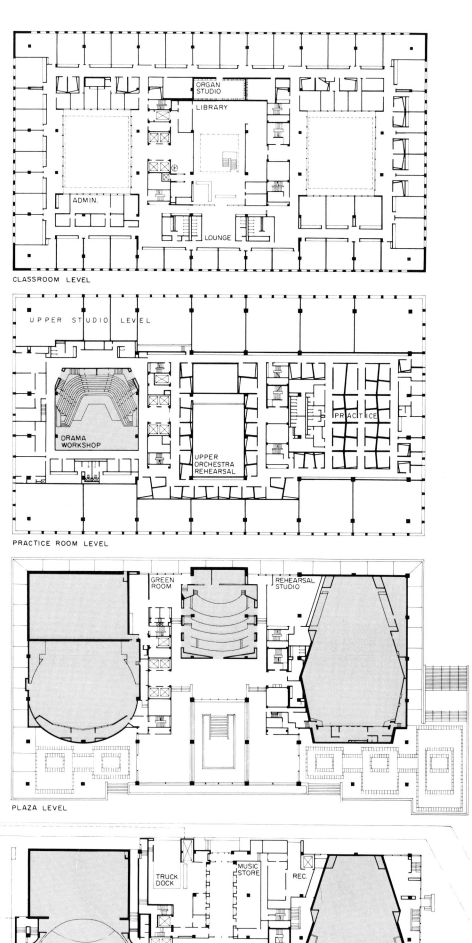

CLASSROOM LEVEL

PRACTICE ROOM LEVEL

PLAZA LEVEL

STREET LEVEL

20

Lounges and lobbies both public and private are generous and well-scaled, but economical in materials and finish. Although the facades are of travertine (a gift) and the floors are carpeted wall-to-wall (wherever appropriate to reduce noise levels) Juilliard is by no means luxurious. Because of rapidly rising costs, finish details were simplified wherever possible throughout the structure and more expensive materials abandoned. The wood paneling, for example, which had been designed for the principal lobbies, was eliminated and the concrete left exposed.

The lobby of Alice Tully Hall (opposite page, top left) has a purple carpet and gold accents. Miss Tully, the donor of the hall, took an active interest in its decor. The Juilliard Theater lobby (top right) is carpeted in crimson. The handsome globe-shaped lighting fixtures are of standard manufacture and are also used in Paul Recital Hall.

The principal lobby (opposite page, bottom) interconnects the Juilliard Theater and Alice Tully Hall. Stairs lead to the Paul Recital Hall directly above.

A handsome room, the Juilliard Theater has an adjustable ceiling designed for opera production and training, yet suitable for drama and dance. The most remarkable feature of this 960-1,026 seat theater is its movable ceiling which adjusts to three positions within a seven-foot range to change the angle of reflection of sound from the stage and pit and reduce the volume (and thereby the reverberation time) of the room for drama, or increase the volume and reverberation time for the performance of music. This ceiling, finished in basswood and cherry to match the sidewalls, forms a sound reflective shell, made of horizontal, overlapping curved and tapered tiers. It includes platforms and light bridges for stage lighting and provides access to all other over-head services. Since the entire structure is located over the audience, safety was of prime importance. The architects and the ceiling engineer Olaf Soöt chose a long-span one-piece structure over several smaller movable units. The selection of a long-span structure on heavier but simple machinery minimized the maintenance requirements, reduced the over-all cost, and provided a fool-proof "fail-safe" system.

The basic structure consists of two main box trusses tied together by box-type secondary trusses. This box truss system forms the self-braced structural support for all the secondary framing, catwalks and ceiling panels. It is supported by four self-locking jackscrews and is held laterally by four guide columns, one near each jackscrew.

Each pair of jackscrews is driven by one main drive assembly. Because of the large distances between each pair of jackscrews, it was impractical to connect the main drives by me-chanical means and, therefore, electrical synchronization with self-compensating leveling at predetermined stops was employed. Should any of the shafts or other drive train compo-nents become disconnected from the associated jackscrew drive, the ceiling will stop and cannot be operated unless the repairs are made. Additional interlock systems protect personnel and machinery. The ceiling is operated from a control station within the auditorium, but for the ceiling to move another button must be kept under constant pressure by an operator located in the catwalks with a full view of the service area.

The stage and lighting facilities of the Juilliard Theater and the three other halls were planned by Jean Rosenthal Associates, Inc. The associate engineer-in-charge was Clyde L. Nordheimer.

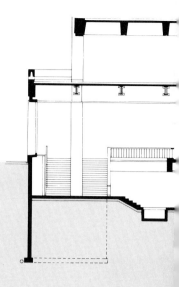

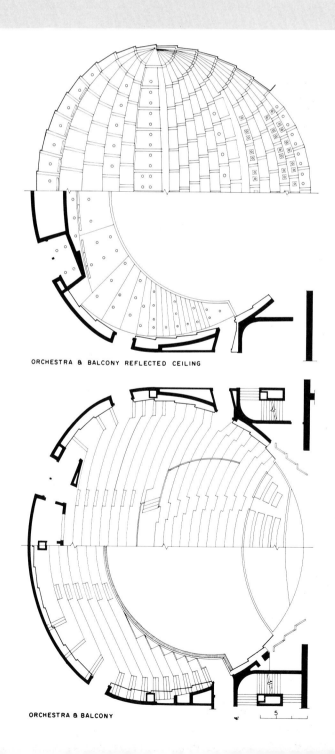

ORCHESTRA & BALCONY REFLECTED CEILING

ORCHESTRA & BALCONY

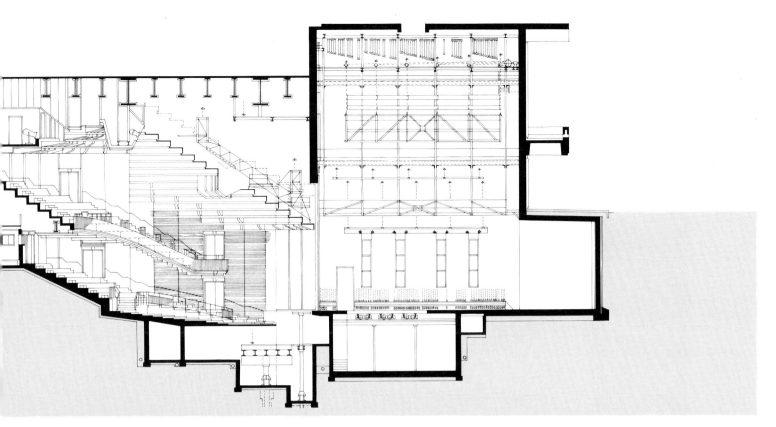

A Lincoln Center facility and Juilliard's only public hall, Alice Tully Hall is designed primarily for recitals and chamber ensembles.

This hall, unlike the Juilliard Theater, is not acoustically adjustable, and therefore cannot approach an ideal for each type of performance which will take place there. Lincoln Center, Juilliard, the architects, and their acoustician Heinrich Keilholz, considered of first importance that the hall meet recital and chamber music requirements. The 1,096-seat hall is not too large for this function and critical response to the acoustics for this type of performance has so far been good. Acoustician Keilholz points out that Tully Hall should not be used by large orchestras, and adds that if the acoustics prove good for other musical purposes than those for which the hall was designed "it will be a gift!" He attributes part of Tully Hall's acoustical success to the use of wood as a resonant material and points out that musicians like to have it around them. Dampening has been inserted where needed behind the wood battens.

The recital stage has a depth of 23 feet and an average width of 50 feet. An organ can be raised into position or lowered and concealed at the rear. For small orchestras an additional 14 feet of stage depth is obtained by stowing the first three rows of seating under the stage and raising a lift to stage level. This configuration will also accommodate modest theatrical performances. Draperies, lighting, pipes and other scenic devices are suspended from electric winch systems above the stage ceiling. The side walls pivot for access from back stage and a traveler curtain can be drawn across the stage.

In addition to the standard concert lighting, Tully Hall is equipped with a complete theatrical lighting system. If an orchestra pit is required, two additional rows of seats can be stored under the stage.

Facilities for film presentations have been designed into the space. A complete projection booth and sound system have been installed.

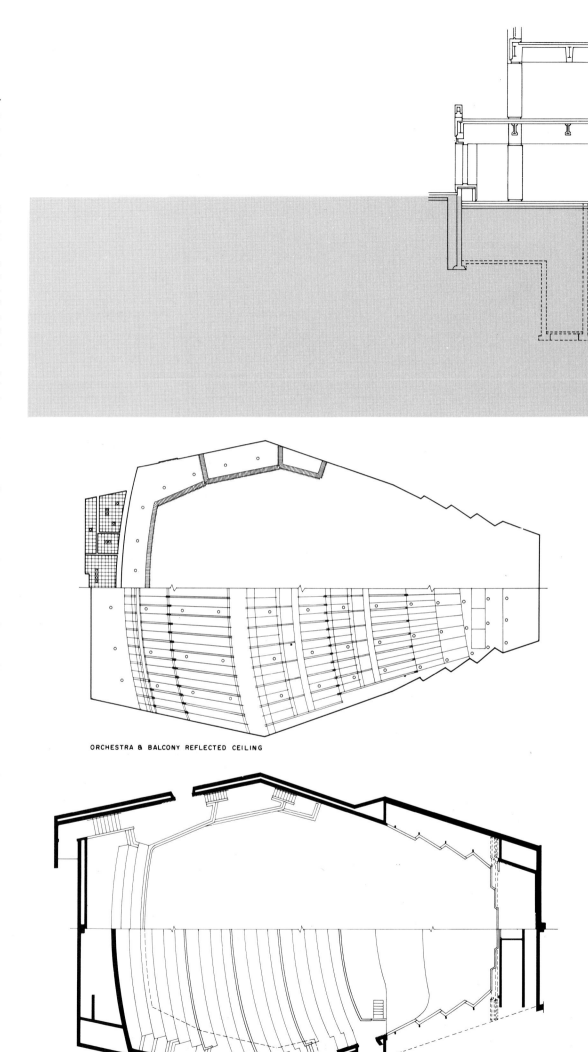

ORCHESTRA & BALCONY REFLECTED CEILING

ORCHESTRA & BALCONY

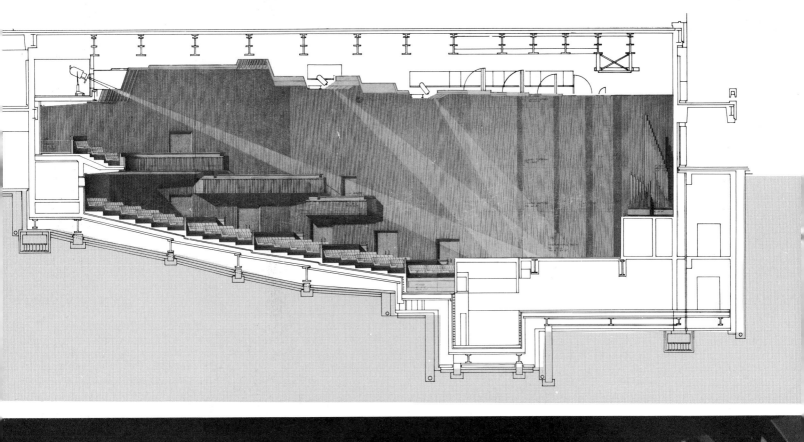

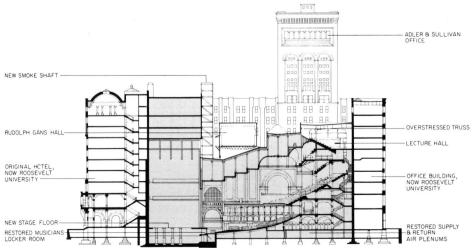

NEW SMOKE SHAFT

RUDOLPH GANS HALL

ORIGINAL HOTEL,
NOW ROOSEVELT
UNIVERSITY

NEW STAGE FLOOR
RESTORED MUSICIANS
LOCKER ROOM

ADLER & SULLIVAN
OFFICE

OVERSTRESSED TRUSS

LECTURE HALL

OFFICE BUILDING,
NOW ROOSEVELT
UNIVERSITY

RESTORED SUPPLY
& RETURN
AIR PLENUMS

A Chicago landmark reminted with care to provide an opulent setting for modern performances

Unlike some of their other buildings, Adler & Sullivan's great Auditorium Theater in Chicago had been badly misused for 25 years before its restoration was begun, but like the Patent Office, it had barely escaped demolition. To bring it back to its original form was more a matter of renovation and repair than of reconstruction, for the building proved, after careful structural inspection and analysis, to be basically sound. One truss was found to have become over-stressed because of settling, and this was strengthened. The stage floor was replaced (it had been used as a bowling alley during World War II when the theater was a USO Center) and new fans and heating and cooling coils were installed to work with the original duct system. The remarkable stage equipment—Adler's genius showed here as in the heating and air conditioning system he devised—was in surprisingly good condition, considering its years of disuse and misuse. New stage lighting was required; new ropes for scenery placement, restoration of some of the hydraulic lifts, new dressing rooms and new plumbing were provided. The major costs, however, were for plaster repair, paint and a new electrical system. There were unexpected rewards for faithful adherence to the original plans: When a row of boxes, installed between the orchestra seats and the grand foyer were removed to restore the continuity between theater area and foyer, excellently preserved examples of the original paint and Sullivan's beautiful stencilling were found. The faithful restoration included new chairs in the original design, a duplication of the red carpet Sullivan had designed, even the same kind of long carbon-filament light bulbs that had made the "Golden Arches" scintillate.

Hedrich-Blessing

The successful restoration of the Auditorium Theater, a demanding and difficult job because of a tight budget, was due to the careful research of the building's original condition, the repair and reconditioning of every possible part of the theater, and the replacement of only those parts (missing plaster ornament, for instance) that could not be repaired.

THE AUDITORIUM THEATER, Chicago, Illinois. Owner: *The Auditorium Theater Council.* Architects: *Adler & Sullivan* (original); *Harry Weese & Associates* (restoration). Engineers: *Severud Associates; The Engineers Collaborative.* Interiors: *Dolores Miller & Associates.* General Contractor: *J. W. Snyder Construction Co.*

A variety of houses, each carefully designed for specific kinds of performances

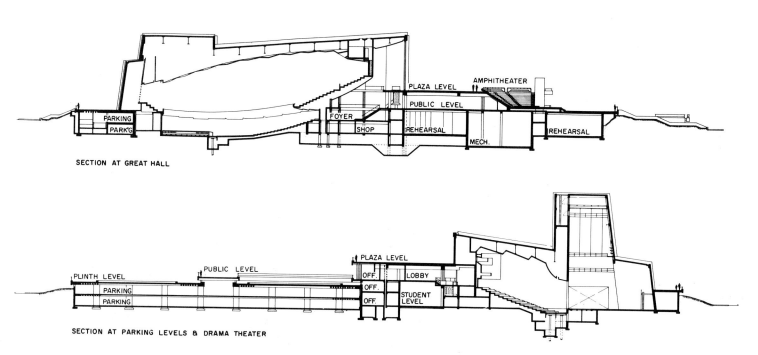

SECTION AT GREAT HALL

SECTION AT PARKING LEVELS & DRAMA THEATER

Hedrich-Blessing photos

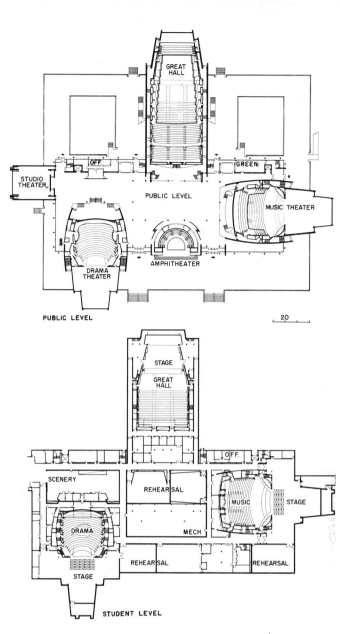

GREAT HALL

OFF. GREEN

STUDIO THEATER

PUBLIC LEVEL

MUSIC THEATER

DRAMA THEATER

AMPHITHEATER

PUBLIC LEVEL

20

STAGE

GREAT HALL

OFF.

SCENERY

REHEARSAL

MUSIC

STAGE

DRAMA

MECH.

REHEARSAL

REHEARSAL

STAGE

STUDENT LEVEL

This $22-million complex, designed by Max Abramovitz with George Izenour as theater equipment consultant and Dr. Cyril M. Harris as acoustician, has been designed to accommodate the teaching and performance requirements of the School of Music, the Department of Theater, the School of Dance and the university bands of the University of Illinois at Urbana–Champaign. It is also a community cultural center serving a large public audience.

An extremely generous private grant from the Krannert family made it possible to build five different facilities each of the optimum size and shape for the types of performance housed. None, for example, require the built-in acoustical and mechanical flexibility of other halls. The facilities include the 2,100-seat Great Hall, or concert hall, designed primarily for orchestral and choral performances, the 985-seat Festival Theater, or music theater for chamber music, intimate opera and musicals, the 678-seat Playhouse, or drama theater, designed for legitimate theater and dance recitals as well as many other kinds of performances, the 150-seat Studio Theater for experimental productions and the 560-seat outdoor amphitheater for open-air musical and dramatic performances.

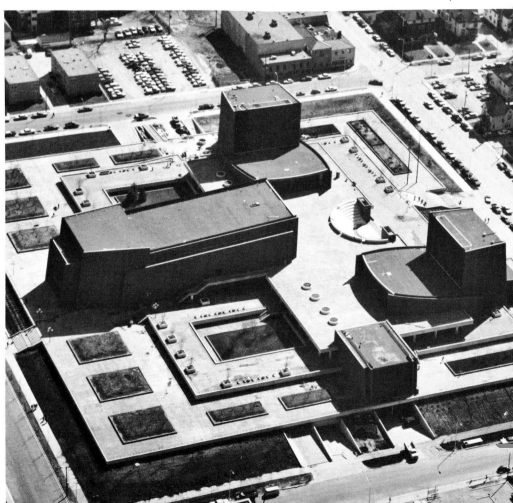

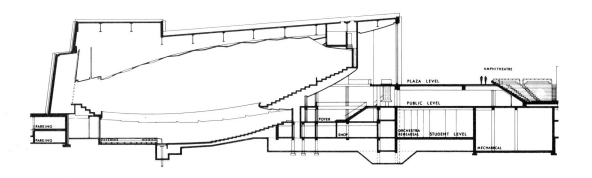

PARKING | PARKING | | FOYER | SHOP | ORCHESTRA REHEARSAL STUDENT LEVEL | MECHANICAL | PLAZA LEVEL | PUBLIC LEVEL | AMPHITHEATRE

The concert hall is rectangular in form and has been designed as one room without a proscenium. Audience and orchestra share the same space. According to Dr. Cyril M. Harris, the acoustical consultant, it is a highly traditional hall, similar in size and shape to Boston's Symphony Hall, Amsterdam's Concertgebouw and several old Viennese halls. The hall is the right size and volume for the unamplified performance of symphonic and choral works although a retractable sound system has been provided in the ceiling. (There was no pressure to build a larger hall since the University of Illinois already possessed a huge assembly hall designed by Abramovitz.) The stage provides ample space for a 120-piece orchestra. When a chorus is required on stage, the latter can be increased in size by a hydraulic lift at its front edge.

The only movable elements are two vertically adjustable walls —one seals off the organ behind the choir and the other conceals the upper tiers of the choir. (The first tier of choir seats remains open so that students may watch the symphony director conduct.)

The 1½-inch-thick plaster ceiling is shaped in an origami pattern to provide maximum diffusion for more uniform distribution of sound and to allow it to fade evenly. This handsome ceiling acts in combination with the surface breaks on the butternut wood sidewalls and on the plaster balcony faces and soffits, to take the place of the columns, pilasters, niches, statues, cartouches, moldings and decorative plaster coffers which are such excellent sound diffusers in the fine concert halls built in the past. In addition, the balcony faces are angled to better reflect the sound for those seated on the orchestra floor.

As the section indicates, the 989-seat balcony overhangs only seven tiers of the 1,111-seat orchestral floor. Its great depth cantilevers into the lobby and foyer spaces—thus there are no deep pockets into which sound either cannot enter or is trapped, and no dead spots in the orchestra seating.

"I'm a believer in wood," says Harris. Not only did he advise its use on the sidewalls but both the stage and orchestra floor are of wood on joists. Sound absorption is provided by people, upholstered seats and a limited use of carpet.

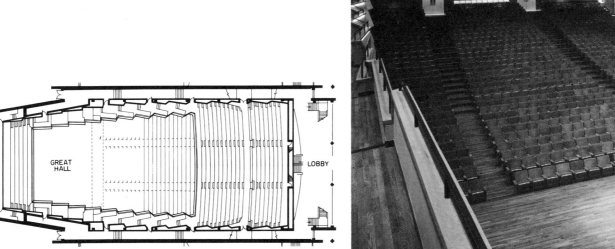

GREAT HALL

LOBBY

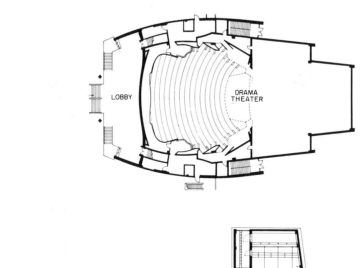

LOBBY

DRAMA
THEATER

PLAZA LEVEL

OFFICE PUBLIC
LOBBY

OFFICE

OFFICE STUDENT LEVEL

The 678-seat drama theater shown at right and in plan and section (left) was shaped to provide the lowest possible cubic volume per seat consistent with other requirements, so that speech can be heard to best advantage. The smaller volume provides a lesser reverberation time and these factors, combined with the use of reflective rather than absorptive surfaces, provide optimum conditions for spoken drama. Only the upholstered seats and the rear wall below the projection booths are absorptive. Ceilings, side walls and the face of the projection booths are of plaster.

The drama theater has steeply banked continental seating providing good sight lines and a sense of closeness to the actors on the stage. The color scheme combines Venetian red seats and smoke blue walls. The stage differs slightly from that of the music theater because of its more elaborate forestage, a portion of which extends into the seating area and can be raised by two hydraulic lifts to serve as a thrust stage or be lowered to accommodate a small orchestra. The proscenium opening is 38 feet wide and there is 30 feet of depth to the cyclorama.

The music theater shown at left and in plan and section (right) has 701 seats downstairs and 264 in the balcony, and except for the fact that it has a balcony is very similar in design to the drama theater. Both halls have a good rake to the seats for sight and sound. The orchestra section of the music theater has two center aisles and two side aisles, while the balcony has continental seating, thus increasing the number of good balcony seats. The balcony is high enough not to block or trap sound under it and its shape helps reflect and diffuse the sound. The hall is painted white and the seats are upholstered in red mohair. The stage of the music theater is large and well equipped. The proscenium arch is 40 feet wide and there is 30 feet of depth to the cyclorama. Two hydraulic lifts can be used to enlarge the apron of the stage. When these lifts are raised, the stage thrusts out into the audience to provide directors with opportunities for many variations in production. The lifts can also be lowered below seating level to make an orchestra pit, which varies in size according to whether one lift or two are used. Idaho white pine covers the stage of the Festival Theater.

A cyclorama, or sky drop, can be lowered into position when needed. This cyclorama is constructed of a translucent material.

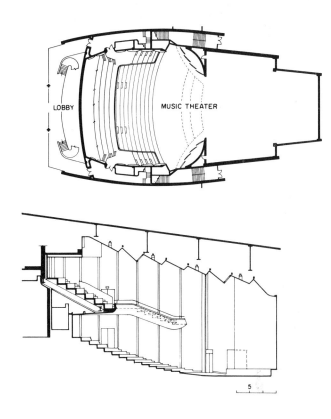

Foyers and lounges isolate the theaters against sound and vibrations. Vertical wooden strips, covering fiberglass absorptive material, form the walls of these areas, and all floors are carpeted. Shown at left (top) is the upper lobby of the concert hall and (bottom) its main foyer tucked under the cantilevered balcony.

KRANNERT CENTER FOR THE PERFORMING ARTS, University of Illinois at Urbana-Champaign, Urbana, Illinois. Architect: *Max Abramovitz of the firm of Harrison & Abramovitz;* structural engineers: *Zetlin, DeSimone, Chaplin & Associates;* mechanical and electrical engineers: *Cosentini Associates;* stage design: *Jo Mielziner;* stage equipment: *George C. Izenour;* acoustics: *Dr. Cyril M. Harris;* landscape: *Sasaki, Dawson, DeMay Associates;* contractor: *Turner Construction Company.*

An art center designed to link two campuses and provide flexible theater space for each

The Paul Mellon Center for the Arts has been conceived both symbolically and literally as a gateway between two Connecticut prep schools—Choate and its newly adopted sister Rosemary. The girls' school moved from Greenwich to become Choate's neighbor at Wallingford in September 1971. While sites for the new building were under consideration, architect Pei urged that the proposed structure become a principal means by which the about-to-be-built campus for girls would be linked to the older campus for boys.

Pei's solution can be quickly grasped by studying the axonometric projection (left) and the bird's-eye photo (below). The new arts complex is essentially two buildings, diagonally bisected by a broad curving pathway surfaced with tile and partially open to the sky, which culminates in a broad staircase. The juxtaposition of the curved and straight transparent walls, the portals and the stair produce an exciting spatial sequence. En route to Choate (above), the interpenetrating assymetric design produces a quite different but still intriguing plastic effect.

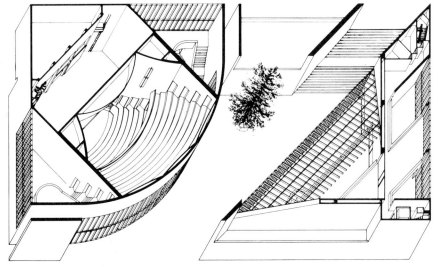

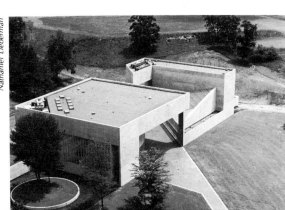

As the top photo (left) partially indicates the arts center has been placed within and looks out upon broad surrounding meadows. These handsome open spaces were created at Pei's insistence from a site originally marred by inferior out buildings and too many nondescript trees.

The lounge (three photos at right) and the auditorium foyer (bottom photo at left) play an important plastic role in the diagonal spatial sequence linking Choate to Rosemary. Physically separated from the path by their transparent glass enclosures, these areas, nonetheless, are strongly connected to the center of things. Students in the lounge and visitors to the auditorium are never out of touch with what is going on along the path.

Originally the lounge was not in the program. Architect Pei, however, thought that the Choate and Rosemary students would need a special place to get together and that the projected arts center would be ideal for this purpose. If a lounge were made adjacent to the theater, art studios and practice rooms, a typical student's interest in art might grow from a first shy attempt to find common ground with the opposite sex. "The building is more than a gateway," says Pei. "It is also a trap, designed to lure the boys and girls to each other and to art." Painting, sculpture and weaving take place on the two cantilevered mezzanines within the lounge as the section (below) indicates. As can also be seen in the section, a portion of the auditorium is underground to bring the roof of the stagehouse in line with the well proportioned cornice height. The auditorium roof, although sheathed in concrete and originally intended to be framed by concrete Verendiel trusses, was finally constructed in steel because of time and budget.

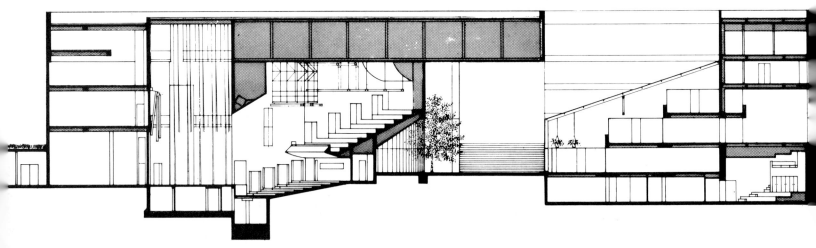

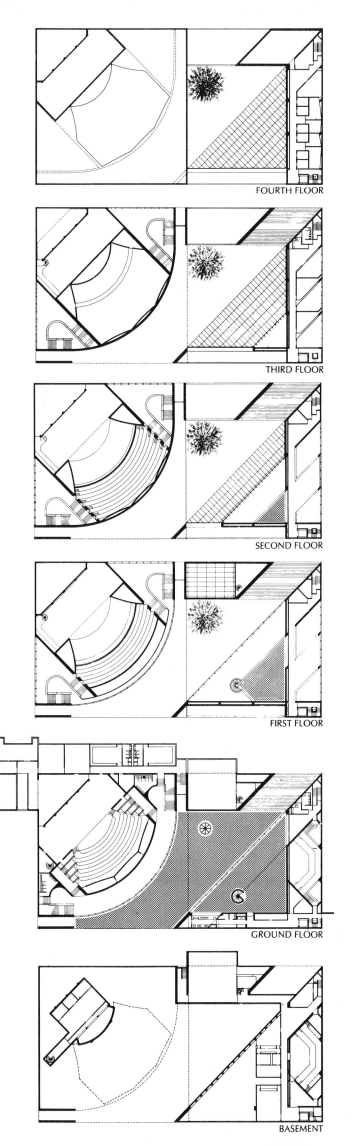

FOURTH FLOOR

THIRD FLOOR

SECOND FLOOR

FIRST FLOOR

GROUND FLOOR

BASEMENT

The arts center has six levels. In the basement of the theater wing are equipment and storage space, the trap room and the orchestra pit. In the teaching wing are the experimental theater and its storage, the recital room, a storage and mechanical room, miscellaneous office spaces and a small library. At the ground floor level are the court or pathway, the orchestra seating, stage and ancillary spaces in the auditorium, the upper level of the recital room in the teaching wing, and the main floor of the lounge. The first floor contains the balcony and its lobby, the first of two lounge mezzanines and the art studios. The second floor consists largely of the upper levels of the first floor spaces and includes the second lounge mezzanine. The third floor has class and seminar rooms in the teaching wing and a mechanical room behind the stage house. The latter room was improperly insulated from the stage because of unfortunate budget cuts, and presently is a source of objectionable noise during rehearsal and performance. On the fourth floor of the teaching wing are music practice rooms and the skylight.

Apart from the difficulties with the mechanical room, the auditorium acoustics work quite well. The room is flexible and expandable. For drama the auditorium seats 840, but the balcony can be closed off to create an intimate 400-seat theater. For music three configurations are available: an 800-seat theater with orchestra pit and full stage house for musicals, an expanded stage with retractable shell for orchestral performances, and a 400-seat intimate hall for recitals and chamber music using the retractable shell.

THE PAUL MELLON ARTS CENTER, Choate School and Rosemary Hall, Wallingford, Connecticut. Architects: *I.M. Pei & Partners—architect-in-charge—Ralph Heisel;* project managers—*John Scarlata and Paul Veeder;* resident architect: *Murray Kalender;* interiors: *Robert Lym;* engineers: *Olaf Soot* (structural); *Campbell and Friedland* (mechanical); theater consultants: *George Izenour Associates;* landscape architect: *Joseph R. Gangemi;* general contractor: *George B. H. Macomber Company.*

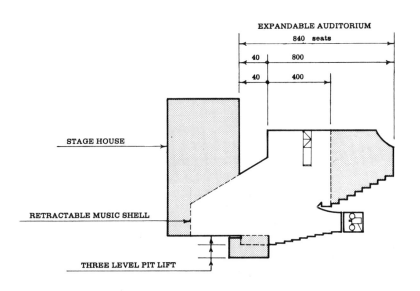

EXPANDABLE AUDITORIUM

840 seats

40 | 800

40 | 400

STAGE HOUSE

RETRACTABLE MUSIC SHELL

THREE LEVEL PIT LIFT

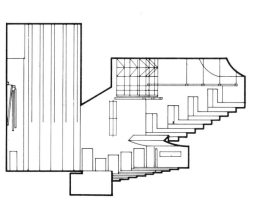

An innovative center
for the performing arts
in Cincinnati's Eden Park

The site of the 672 seat Robert S. Marx Theater is a grassy knoll located in downtown Cincinatti's Eden Park. Where it faces the plaza the new building appears small and in scale with its Victorian neighbor. The stainless steel roofs slope gently downward to reduce the height of walls which enclose the upper portion of lobby, backstage and shop areas. These walls, also of stainless steel, are a reflective surface presenting a shimmering image of the Victorian pavilion and the movement of people across the plaza. Airport taxiway lights of the standard beautiful blue, used in combination with incandescent bulbs in exposed porcelain sockets and wire cages, light the plaza at night. Architect Hardy has the pop artist's knack of taking familiar and prosaic objects and using them in fresh ways. For the first time these objects become beautiful or curious or funny—but as used by Hardy they are never wholly capricious. The five-level lobby is another diverting exercise in the transformation and exaltation of the mundane, and as such is an appropriately contemporary background for theater-goers. If in the future, as fashions change, this lobby is left as it is (as it should be), it will stand as an unrepentant period piece of the late sixties. Lowly ducts and air diffusers, hidden or screened until now, have become works of sculpture in stainless steel. Clusters of chrome-shielded fluorescent tubes, usually semi-concealed, are here exposed in all their nakedness in great vertical chandeliers. Even incandescent warehouse floodlights are used. Mirrors become a means to fracture space, to dissolve its edges and to create unexpected visual relationships and juxtapositions. And carpet is on the ceilings as well as the floors. Again this is no mere caprice. The carpet effectively lowers the noise level in this lobby.

Norman McGrath photos

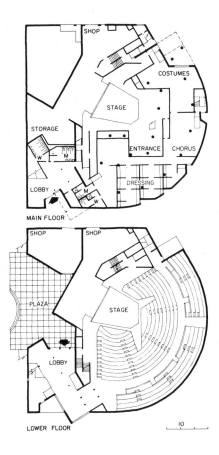

SHOP
COSTUMES
STAGE
STORAGE
W M M
ENTRANCE CHORUS
M
LOBBY
DRESSING
W
MAIN FLOOR

SHOP SHOP
PLAZA
STAGE
LOBBY
LOWER FLOOR 10

The asymmetrical thrust stage can be entered by the actors from any one of twenty-four points to accommodate the style of production favored by theater director Brooks Jones. According to architect Hardy, Jones had strong ideas from the beginning about what he wanted to do: "Brooks had thought through the style of production and the relationship of the audience to the performers and what the quality of the room was supposed to be and do. He wanted what we call the 'bookend' concept, which to us means that when you are in a big amphitheater room you don't look at the stage wall straight on, you look down at the floor and the back wall. What you see is the floor and the wall together. Included within the audience's sightlines are the sidewalls, which we did not want to treat as decorative surfaces to attract attention to themselves. We tried to make these walls work for the performance to give as many ways as possible to get onto the stage. Every conceivable means of entry to

that magic space was provided, and that's the reason why there are all those levels and holes and projections.

"In the beginning Brooks was opposed to an asymmetrical stage, but we as architects disagreed. Our point was that once you put a performance into a room with an audience, the performance becomes a three-dimensional thing which depends on movement as much as speech. There should be the opportunity to move in all sorts of ways which an asymmetrical stage provides. This led to the decision to surround the stage with a pit giving access at any point on its perimeter, not just from the vomitories. In Brooks' style of production actors and audience do not intermix—he thinks this demeans the actor. He wants actors to be larger-than-life-sized people. This was a further reason for cutting the stage off from the audience. The seating bowl doesn't touch the side walls either, except at the points where the audience enters and exits.

"Above all, we wanted to

make sure that the auditorium had the quality of hard 'back-stageness'—that the only space to be soft and fuzzy would be where the audience sits."

To this end the architects not only exposed the building's structural and mechanical systems to full view within the auditorium, but also all the elements which are necessary to theater work. Lighting positions, catwalks, ladders—all are thoroughly revealed.

Upholstered seats with carpeted aisles and the audience itself provide the necessary sound dampening.

ROBERT S. MARX THEATER, Cincinnati. Owner: *Playhouse in the Park Corporation*. Architects: *Hardy Holzman Pfeiffer Associates*; supervising architect: *Robert Habel-Hubert M. Garriot Associates*; structural engineers: *Miller-Tallarico-McNinch & Hoeffel*; mechanical engineers: *Maxfield-Edwards-Backer & Associates*; acoustical engineers: *Robert A. Hansen Associates*; contractors: *Turner Construction Company*.

A remodelled carriage house provides Newark with a small theater for dance

The rehabilitation of carriage houses, in those communities lucky enough to have them, for residential use began as soon as the automobile replaced the horse-drawn carriage. As in most residential work, the architectural and legal problems are relatively simple. But when the carriage house is converted to public use, as was this one at the Newark Community Center of the Arts, the designer must deal with code requirements as stringent as those for new construction of the same type. Thus, a building of 2,000 square feet must accommodate two means of egress, provide adequate toilets, and meet the same codes as larger structures.

Hardy, Holzman and Pfeiffer Associates, architects for the renovation, have met those restrictions with their customary flair. With a limited budget and area in which to work, they have provided rehearsal and performance space for music and dance which works well and admirably captures the spirit of the school. Mrs. David Lass and Saunders Davis, music teachers in the Newark school system, established the Center in January, 1968. Enrollment grew so rapidly that new quar-

ters were needed within six months. Grants from two foundations enabled the school to move into a large house in a once well-to-do Newark neighborhood. Soon afterwards the architects began the conversion of the carriage house behind.

Although the roof and some of the masonry of the existing building had to be replaced, the 20-foot-wide shell dictated the proportions of the revised design. The alley facade (top of the plan, opposite page) remains as it was with all new construction toward the house (which now contains offices and music rehearsal rooms). Performance-goers pass through the house into a courtyard, which will be developed as an outdoor theater, across which they see the sprightly elevation at left. A split-level entrance leads down to toilets and mirrored rehearsal room with an elegant two-position barre and new hardwood floor. The stairs up bring audiences directly into a large room divided diagonally into stage and seating areas. Faced with a 2:5 plan proportion, the architects felt that the diagonal stage permitted the width necessary for dance movement, as a standard stage across one end would not, while not spreading the audience the entire length of the space. A new roof structure echoes and reinforces the stage angle while a clerestory over the audience increases the sense of enclosure about the stage. Performers can come onto the stage from a ramp leading to the lower floor or can enter from an alcove over the lobby. An adjustable stage lighting system adds a glamorous note.

NEWARK COMMUNITY CENTER OF THE ARTS, Newark, New Jersey. Architects: *Hardy, Holzman and Pfeiffer Associates;* general contractor: *Verfield Construction Company, Inc.*

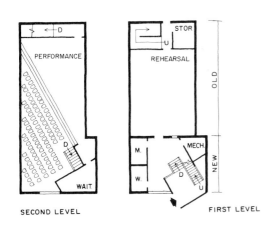

PERFORMANCE

WAIT

SECOND LEVEL

STOR

REHEARSAL

OLD

M. | MECH.

W. | D

NEW

FIRST LEVEL

Mystery, romance and nostalgic evocations of the recent past

Located at the rear of a neighborhood shopping center, this movie theater utilizes long, narrow spaces effectively to control circulation and dampen sound transmission. To psychologically reinforce the need for quiet, the architects have used dark colors (deep blue and charcoal gray) in the waiting areas. Bare bulbs, reflecting off Mylar surfaces, are used to extend the space visually and to create an exciting pattern of lighting accents. A wall mural in the lobby, abstracted into black and white by the removal of all gray tones, depicts a smiling face familiar to a recent generation of movie goers. Supernumerals, in an *art deco* style, mark the sections of the theater and recall for an earlier generation of moviegoers the glamorous stars of Hollywood in the 1930s.

The happy combination of light, color and graphics, all used inventively, stimulates immense visual interest and prepares the viewer for the world of mystery and romance he is about to enter.

BROADVIEW CINEMA I, Savannah, Georgia. Owner: *Weis Theaters, Inc.* Architects: *Arkhora Associates, Inc.—H. Anthony Smith,* partner-in-charge; graphics consultant: Nanci Williams; contractor: *Nelson-Smith.*

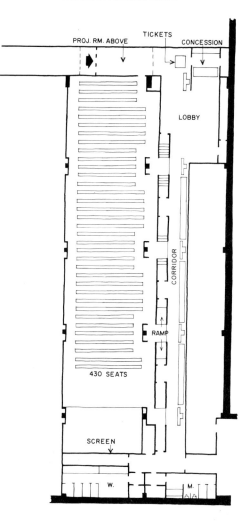

Robin Johnstone photos

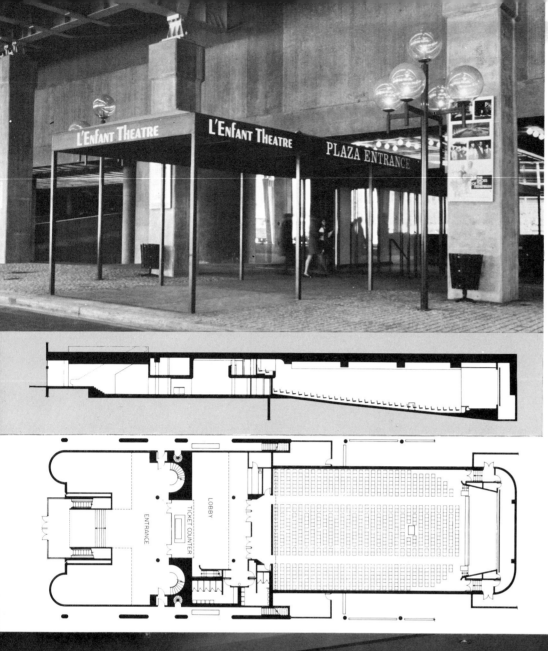

A sophisticated space in Washington, D. C. designed for a variety of film presentations

The restrained, warm elegance of its design is extremely appropriate for this highly sophisticated theater which is used as a multi-media communications center by day and as a cinema in the evening. Among its remarkable array of electronic equipment is a color TV system which will receive, project and simultaneously transmit both picture and sound through a Comsat satellite link-up. The lobby, canopied by sparkling, clear incandescent globes, serves as a reception area and extra viewing space for slides and films. A quiet color scheme of black, beige and walnut, with four shades of purple in upholstery, is repeated in the very simple but effective auditorium. Stuart Pertz was associate in charge for the Jan Pokorny office; Ben Schlanger was consultant; Flack & Kurtz were mechanical engineers; and Tuckman Barbee was contractor.

© Ezra Stoller (ESTO) photos

INTERIORS FOR LIVING

Residential design, during this five year period, continued with diminishing force in the divergent directions laid out a generation before by masters like Le Corbusier and Frank Lloyd Wright. The Miesian tradition of steel and glass houses, however, seemed to end rather abruptly—at least in its pure form—perhaps because architects and owners found its classical formulas limiting and its rigid formalities inimical to contemporary lifestyles.

Richard Meier's house in Eastern Long Island (page 200) represents an extension of several of Le Corbusier's precepts and is rooted in a Mediterranean tradition of white, planar surfaces expressed in sharply disciplined relationships and animated by a system of painted pipe railings bent in ways that express movement and thrust. Finishes and craftsmanship are of the utmost importance here because the joining of planes is articulated with extreme care and little is concealed from view by molding, pipe collars or trim. The structural grid is respected even when it produces a column that falls right in the middle of the living room's main seating area. The interiors also achieve a sculptured quality through the exciting manipulation of space and the designer's skill in turning the fireplace, stairs and patterns of fenestration into powerful sculptural compositions.

The house (page 212) by Charles Gwathmey and Robert Siegel, also in Eastern Long Island, though individual in its own right, clearly belongs to this same design tradition.

Norman Jaffe's design for a beach house (page 208) has very different genes. Unlike the Meier and Gwathmey-Siegel houses, which are sited and massed as man-made objects set in contrast to the natural landscape, Jaffe's house is fitted to its site as if it were a natural extension of the dune. The house is a conscious effort at harmony. Inside and out, natural materials, seldom painted, reaffirm this harmony by celebrating their own beauty and function.

The house by William Turnbull and Charles Moore (page 220), is a "just plain vanilla" house that here represents a body of architectural thought that places a special premium on simple, vernacular expression. Perhaps, it is a reaction against a decade of self-conscious form-giving in residential design. In any case, it is a barn restated and a summation of those unassuming virtues that have always given vernacular buildings their honest and appealing character.

In general, houses have become more informal and relaxed, both in plan and in the manner in which they are furnished. Diagonal spatial relationships in the form of splayed walls and shed roofs re-entered the design vocabulary and new products and materials, particularly plastics, have found increasing acceptance with both architects and owners.

Regionalism continues to disappear and when it emerges in single examples, here or there, it is too often regarded by other architects as a design deceit—a conscious effort at the picturesque or a failure to acknowledge the universal impact of heating and air-conditioning on building design. Where regionalism lingers, it is most often in residual forms—as in Patricia Coplans excellent house for herself (page 222)—where bay windows recall an old San Francisco tradition.

But in spite of the dogged persistence of some formal design philosophies, residential design still provides enormous diversity, serves as an extraordinary challenge to an architect's power of invention, and still offers a crucible in which old ideas can be melted down and minted afresh for use in other houses and, perhaps more important, in other building types.

Ezra Stoller photos ® ESTO

An eloquent arrangement of glass and wood volumes for a large and active family

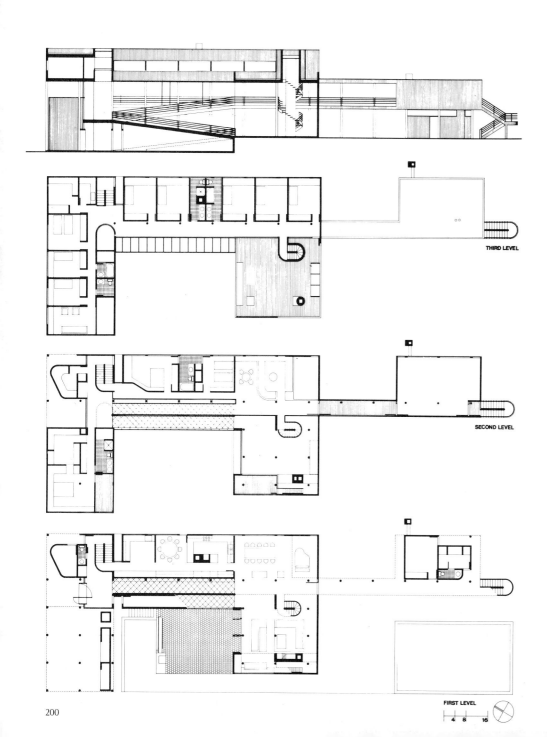

THIRD LEVEL

SECOND LEVEL

FIRST LEVEL

4 8 16

Not many architects produce houses that illuminate philosophic concepts at the same time that they solve esthetic and programmatic problems. Richard Meier does. There is a clarity in Meier's work that compels every architect, no matter what his bias, to study the buildings and absorb the lessons each offers. This house near New York for a family with six children is worth study on four levels: First, as it responds to the work and thought of Le Corbusier. Second, as it conveys the special delight of architectural sculpture. Third, as a thoughtful solution of the clients' program on a specific site. Fourth, as a series of details which solve house-building problems economically and well. In short, it is a very comprehensive approach to residential design.

Richard Meier believes that every architect working today has been affected by Le Corbusier. In his own work, and particularly this house, he cites Corbusier's interest in structural clarity, of the relationship of the horizontal plane to its columnar support and the ensuing visual framework. He cites the bold expression of vertical circulation patterns, such as the ramp, and their incorporation as major design elements. Finally, he cites the play of light and shadow upon form. That is, after all, one of the principal ways in which Le Corbusier defined architecture.

And it is in this way that Meier has particularly succeeded

here. As in his earlier houses, Meier has carefully balanced interior daylight level with the exterior light. Thus, even in the daytime (when many glass buildings become solid mirrored volumes), there is a transparency that is reminiscent of Corbu's tropical buildings—those at Chandigarh or the mill owners' building at Ahmedabad. In other words, in a climate that requires tightly composed and completely enclosed buildings, Meier has achieved the apparent openness of an unenclosed building. That has been the main esthetic quest of a generation of architects:

The illuminated building at twilight (left) conveys the quality well, but transparency in daylight is the true test. With admirable bravura, the architect has used ramps to connect four levels and has underlined their presence with quasi-industrial detailing such as the welded pipe railings and the arched metal glazing structure. The juxtaposition of the arched glass wall and the two glass walls of the living room produces a visual depth that has eluded most designers.

It is this transparency, of course, that makes the house truly sculptural in contemporary terms. It is not enough, today, for external massing to be powerful or pleasing. In both sculpture and architecture there ought to be an interplay of internal and external spaces: a topological continuity is the ideal. Set as an object in a meadow,

The living room is a two-story glazed pavilion, partly defined by the winding metal stair (right) that continues up to the bedrooms on the third level. Yet the space is contiguous with the circulation spine on both levels and with the areas beyond: dining and music below and children's recreation above. Specially-designed white lacquered wood furniture grouped around the fireplace provides a remarkably intimate area for entertaining. The steep stairway behind the fireplace (above) leads to a small deck. From the interior, the deck provides a smaller-scale sitting area to one side of the fireplace. From the exterior, it creates a well-proportioned opening, with the upper glass thoroughly shaded, thus assuring transparency.

the scale of the house is deceiving. The linear quality, so obvious in the second level plan, is largely achieved by the connected pool house/playroom. The total length on that level is almost 160 feet but the house itself is only 85 feet long. Thus, using a swimming pool and ancillary structures, Meier has maximized the thrust of the form into the site.

It is a large house—eleven bedrooms—but it definitely has a residential scale. When the six children are at home with their friends, and young visitors are very frequent, the ramps are alive with running, shouting youngsters. It is an indoor playground. A device which architects have always identified with monumentality, or at least with access for the handicapped, is used here to express an open and informal style of living. Although the plan organization of the house indicates a compartmentalization usually identified with much larger buildings, the intensity of use (a dozen people live here after all) requires such zoning.

Finally, in spite of its steel frame, this is a wood house which owes as much to American house-building techniques as it does to European formal traditions. The 4 ft.-6 in. wide ramp is wood framed, and, like most of the floors, is of dark-stained oak boards. This material, played against glass and white walls inside and out, adds a warmth that is pleasing and entirely appropriate.

The ramps in the acrylic-glazed gallery are the most compelling architectural feature of the house. Framed with 2 by 12's and surfaced with dark-stained oak flooring, their springiness helps to give a domestic scale to what might seem an inappropriately monumental design element. The entry (right) with its red, assymmetrically-pivoted door, leads immediately to the ramp which ascends to the living room (above right). The second leg of the ramp lands above the entry, adjacent to the master bedroom. There, a cylindrical two-story space (right and far right) is topped with a flat skylight.

A spectacular townhouse, framed in steel and glass, provides its owners with unusual amenities and dramatic spatial excitement

Paul Rudolph has introduced a number of spatial and planning innovations and surprises into his design for this New York townhouse. Behind an elegantly disciplined, and somewhat sober facade (brown-painted steel set with obscure, brown, structural glass panels), one enters into a skillfully lighted, white-gray-black series of spaces that culminate in a big, 27-foot-high living area backed by a three-story greenhouse. Level changes, balconies, open stairs, and tidily integrated fittings abound, in Rudolph's typical fashion, to create a lot of variety and interest in a very cohesive series of spaces.

The house was built on the existing frame of an 1870 coach house, which originally had three floors. A fourth level was achieved in the new house, and within the original space, by creating a mezzanine for the master bedroom suite and its adjoining sitting-room balcony.

The usual back garden—one of the great pleasures in a townhouse—has been raised to the top level; greenery and a great sense of openness have been introduced into the living area by skylights and the tall greenhouse. Mirrored walls line the lower portions of the greenhouse to augment the effect and the apparent depth. A balcony-bedroom (which can be closed by folding panels) also overlooks the greenhouse, and is connected by a bridge to the game room level. An open stair connects the living area with the master bedroom suite, and an elevator and a central stair connect all levels.

Floors on the entire first level are surfaced with black slate, and the slate is continued around the dropped living room area as a sill for sitting or counter space.

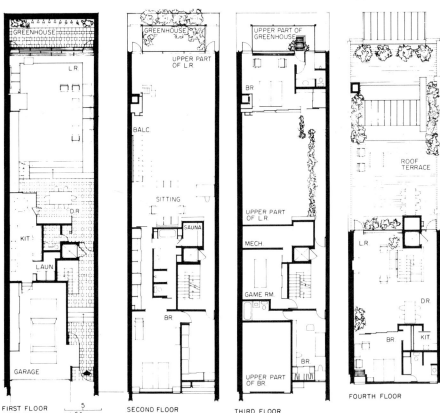

FIRST FLOOR   SECOND FLOOR   THIRD FLOOR   FOURTH FLOOR

Floors in all other areas are covered with gray carpet, with the exception of baths, which are white marble or ceramic tile.

With a lot of the seating and storage built into the house, other furnishings are kept to a minimum, and carefully selected or designed to add to the overall spatial effect. Materials and fabrics are generally kept in the same monochrome color scheme (white-gray-black) as the house, with accents of glass, clear plastic and silver to add sparkle; plants, books and works of art give bright color relief.

Architect: PAUL RUDOLPH
54 West 57th Street, New York City
Townhouse
Location: New York City
Interior design: Paul Rudolph
Contractor: Blitman Corporation

A quiet color scheme and a minimum number of different materials provide a counterfoil to the vigorous changes of level in the big living area. Balconies and bridges extend into the space to create extra usable areas. Stairs are kept to a minimal center support and treads; the slate landing of the stair at right extends to form a mantel for the fireplace.

STUDY   BR

FOURTH LEVEL

GALLERY   D.R.

THIRD LEVELS

BR.

STUDY

SECOND LEVEL

BR.

BR.

FIRST LEVEL

Powerfully shaped dune house for oceanfront site

The strong, contained forms of this beach house by Norman Jaffe reflect a remarkable arrangement of interior spaces within—many levels to effectively zone the house into activity areas, and windows unusually placed to provide panoramic, and sometimes unexpected views. The basic shape of the house is consciously geared to its site. Architect Jaffe comments that, "the site is a dune, a capricious cross section of sand meeting water, subject to the winds and the shifting of the tides. The shape of the dune is permissive, demanding a structure with a stance of its own: the 'feet' of the house are column extensions of wooden piles driven to below sea level on the land side of the dune; the columns continue up to become a roof returning to overhang the openings facing the ocean; the roof on the land side turns downward echoing the sliding return of the dune."

All this is sheathed—roof and walls—in cedar shakes, which helps to both unify and dramatize the sculptural qualities of the protrusions and insets of the design. To anchor the house solidly to its site, rough-hewn granite is used as a podium, extended to form an entrance court and retaining wall for the living room terrace at the top of the dune.

The lowest of the levels which zone the house contains the entry and childrens' rooms. The latter have a separate entrance and little terrace on the east facade of the house (photo bottom left). A free-standing stair leads up one-half level to an area for guests, with bedroom, studio and bath. Spiraling above this are the living areas (living room, dining room, kitchen and gallery), each of which are a few steps above the other. The top level contains the master bedroom, studio, bath, and a deck which cantilevers over the crest of the dune.

Very out-of-the-ordinary windows are used to give daylight and good views to this rising succession of spaces. At the front of the house, a large window is notched into the facade to give a long down-slope vista from the main stair, and another window/skylight is set into front wall and roof to give sky views and light to both a guest room (photo below center) and to the higher-level gallery leading to the master bedroom floor (see section overleaf). Extra light is given to the gallery by a long skylight over the living room. The main living rooms have wide banks of sliding glass walls facing the ocean, as does the master bedroom.

The combination of the unusually placed and sized windows, the projections of the various cantilevers, and the skin-like "wrapping" of cedar shakes give the relatively small house an arresting, and eye-deceiving sense of monumental scale without compromise to its overall sense of warmth and comfort.

Architect Jaffe has used some of the level changes in the Perlbinder house for innovative purposes. The step-up to the dining area, for example, is used to frame a built-in sofa, and the floor of the gallery level forms a generous sink-counter for the kitchen. The gallery also extends as a sitting balcony overlooking the living and stair areas.

As on the exterior, a single material helps weld all the levels together: all of the walls, ceilings, cabinets and built-in furniture are Douglas fir, and the floors are either of the same material or of Pennsylvania slate.

Bill Maris photos

Architect: Norman Jaffe, New York *Associate:* Michael Wolfe *Location:* Sagaponac, Long Island, New York *Structural engineer:* James Romeo *Contractor:* Stephen Perlbinder

Careful modulation of spaces and innovative details for a handsome penthouse in New York

To organize the functions and regulate the flow of spaces in this handsome Manhattan penthouse, architect Stephen Kiviat has made use of built-ins, half-height partitions and changes of level. These design devices have also afforded him an opportunity for some innovative detailing. The dropped soffit and marble sill that wrap around two sides of the living room, for instance, provide a continuous track for plastic picture mounts. The owner, an enthusiastic print collector, can change his prints easily by lifting the plastic mount, substituting the new print, then lowering the mount into position in the track again.

In both living room and bedroom—where a bed surround provides additional storage—lighting is carefully controlled so that it may highlight wall displays and dramatize the apartment's forceful sculptural character. Warm browns and muted earth colors in leather and paint form a low-key contrast to white walls and are exceptionally easy to live with.

PRIVATE RESIDENCE, New York City. Architects: *Kiviat-Rappoport (Stephen H. Kiviat, partner-in-charge)*; contractor: *Glen Partition Company.*

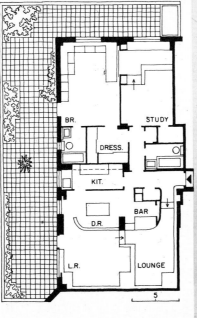

Alexandre Georges photos

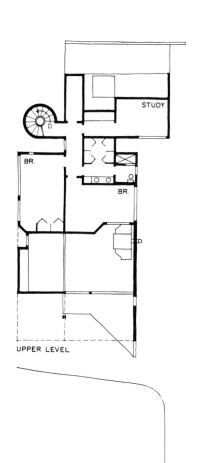

UPPER LEVEL

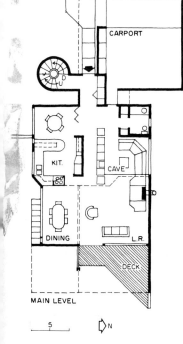

MAIN LEVEL

5   N

LOWER LEVEL

Supergraphics enrich an already forceful design scheme

The Lauren Studebaker House, winner of the Seattle Times "Home of the Year" for 1970, is located in a deciduous forest setting on Mercer Island, Washington. Three distinctive red cedar-clad forms dominate the uneven terrain. They consist of two hard-edged angular volumes penetrated playfully by expanses of glass and a third, the cylindrical sky-lit stairwell.

According to Wendell Lovett, its architect, the house was planned "for varying activities and moods of a young family of five." This was accomplished

with great sensitivity by relating the internal functions to various solar exposures. Southerly oriented rooms are generally for active pursuits while the northern spaces tend to be quiet and individualized. A dynamic visual enrichment is exploited with vistas of the east and south channel of Lake Washington which vary with the season.

Further zoning which adds to the spatial variety occurs vertically on three levels: communal and family activities located on mid- or entry-level; children's rooms expressed in a day-

light basement with playrooms opening onto a terrace; and adult sleeping located on the top level for maximum privacy.

The warm character of the natural materials used outside, is carried inside as a reflection of a totally enveloping experience.

Architect: WENDELL H. LOVETT. *Owners:* Mr. and Mrs. Lauren Studebaker. *Location:* Mercer Island, Washington. *Engineer:* Richard Stern (mechanical). *Landscape architects:* Sakuma/James. *Contractor:* S. G. Moshier and Sons.

Christian Staub photos

The projecting fireplace is clearly the focal point of the Studebaker House. On one side is the enclosed and cozy center for family activities, nick-named the "cave" by the architect. On the other is the spacious and open living-dining room. The cave is enlivened by a handsome activity wall containing audio-visual equipment. The breakfast room and kitchen (above) are equally well-detailed with the same lively character. The living-dining room, on the other hand, relies on a soaring wood ceiling and natural vistas for a more serene atmosphere.

A large Long Island house of unusual comfort and visual enrichment

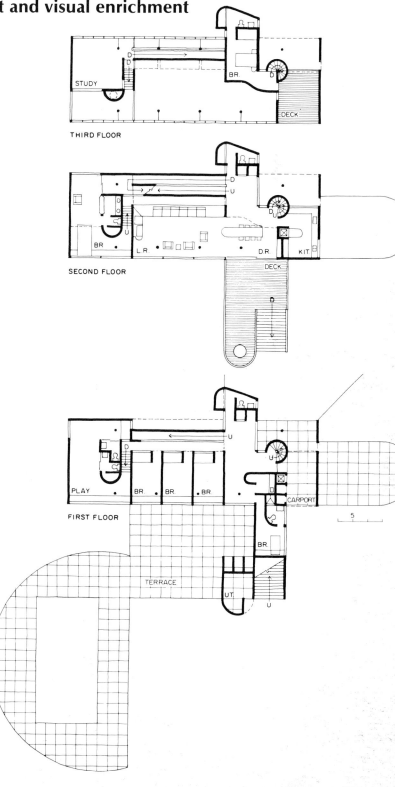

THIRD FLOOR

SECOND FLOOR

FIRST FLOOR

East Hampton, for some time a busy bazaar for contemporary architectural experiments (both superb and otherwise), now has a new attention-getter: the lean, powerful elegance of this sizable house synthesizes some of today's design directions—and with great aplomb.

The house is very much in the stylistic vein of this architectural firm's work, and demonstrates a continuing growth in assurance and maturity. It is a country house of great comfort, privacy and livability—qualities which sometimes get diluted in the architect's quest for design purity and unity.

The house sits like a big, artfully asymmetrical sculpture on a gently sloping five-acre site. It is bounded on the south by a pond, with views of the ocean beyond. To take full advantage of these vistas, the living-dining areas are elevated, European fashion, to the second floor. The ground floor level, below, is zoned by an entry which separates car and service areas from bedrooms for the family's three children and their adjoining indoor and outdoor play spaces. On varying levels above the main living spaces are ranged the master bedroom suite, a study, guest accommodations and a roof terrace; all are connected by a ramp and by stairs. Thus, each activity area of the house has its own "zone" and full privacy.

The structure has a regular column grid of white-painted steel which supports the basically rectangular roof. The rest of the structure is wood frame, clad inside and out with tongue-and-groove cedar siding treated with a bleaching oil to obtain a soft gray color. All cabinet work is treated as a "secondary building system" and is also surfaced in white. The basic rectangle of the house is

relieved by what the architects describe as "variations in erosions, transparencies and extensions related to views, indoor-outdoor, public and private activities." The resulting interplay of geometric voids and solids, great stairs and elevated pipe-railed terraces has a strong recall of the "International Style" of the 1930s; it is an approach to design which works well in such a big-scaled house as this without seeming pretentious or overbearing.

But the house is very much of today, especially in its amenities—including a very well handled and integrated automobile approach and carport (there is even a dumbwaiter to transport groceries to the second-level kitchen). The house has electric heating and cooling, kitchen and laundry equipment, built-in intercom and hi-fi systems. Quality is good throughout, and the cost was about $35 per square foot including cabinet work and carpet.

The landscaping and interior design for the house were also done by the architects, and contribute enormously to the visual cohesiveness and unity of the place. Daylighting has been as carefully considered as artificial light for night; clerestories and skylights add balance and drama, and operable canvas awnings shade the big living area window wall. All interiors are furnished in a generously scaled, low key, comfortable fashion with spots of bright color for accent against the basic gray of the bleached cedar siding and white monochrome of the skeletal steel structure and detailing.

Architects: GWATHMEY SIEGEL ARCHITECTS. *Location:* East Hampton, New York. *General contractor:* John Caramagna.

213

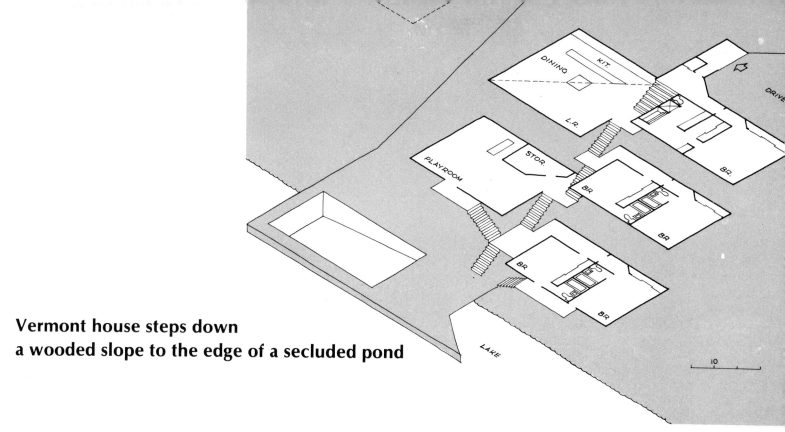

Vermont house steps down a wooded slope to the edge of a secluded pond

Norman McGrath photos

A cool secluded pond is the focus for this house in the Green Mountains of Vermont. Access by car is possible only at a level 35 feet above the water, and so the entrance is at the top and the house is a series of terraced rooms facing the view and arranged around a central stairway that steps down inexorably from the entrance to the pond below, and just before (for the less adventurous) to an open deck and swimming pool.

Exigency as well as predilection controlled some of the decisions, too, for the house is made of standard 2 by 4 framing, with standard windows, doors, skylights, and commonly available sizes of plywood and sheetrock, installed with a minimum of cutting.

The architect points out that he was trying to put standard parts together in other than standard ways. This, admittedly, is not a unique intention today, as anything that veers even a single degree from the standard can skew the construction budget out of all recognition. Here, though, the attempt has worked: the house is not standard, and certainly doesn't look standard.

The long stairway, covered over by a 57-foot skylight, is a critical element among the special qualities of the house. From the outside, it helps bring the separate rooms together to make a single shape, and from the inside it performs a similar function. Flooded with sunlight, it allows movement up and down and across it, and even provides a place—an interior garden in the center of the house—for temporary repose; or for catching a passing glimpse of the sky or the water below.

Architect: PETER L. GLUCK. *Owners:* Mr. and Mrs. B. Bookstaver. *Location:* Westminster, Vermont.

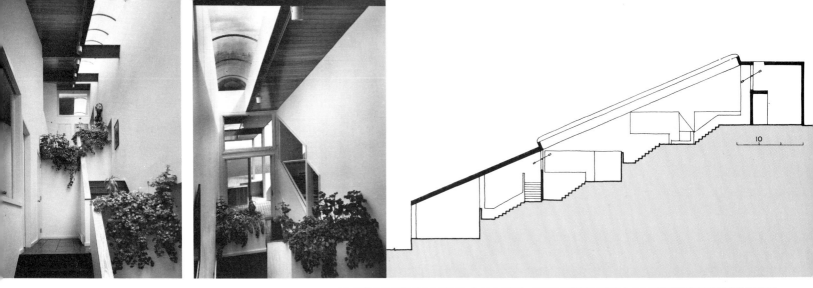

Near the entrance at the top of the house, the stairway opens directly into the living room (left), which is also seen on the right and above. The long skylight above the stairs allows solar heat generated in this space to rise to the top and exit through a large pivot window, creating a chimney effect. Outside air is drawn into the house from below, resulting in a natural air-conditioning system.

Vernacular forms used with sophistication and skill

A. Youngmeister photos

This ingenious vacation house has been built well over a dozen times at the Sea Ranch in California. The basic notion is simplicity itself: a barn-like space with a plan that can be flipped and with an appended lean-to whose function is variable. The working out of the notion, though, assures that simplicity does not lead to dullness.

The ground floor plan is circuitous, so that the apparent size of the space is increased because the eye can never see all of it at once. The "Z" shaped plan of the second floor allows sunlight to fall into the living areas from skylights in the roof, casting patterns that change with the hours and the seasons. It also provides upward vistas from below, and the pleasure of moving from a low space, like the dining area, to one that is dramatically higher. One can also move outside the enclosing walls of the house to lounge in a bay window, or right up to the peak of the roof to doze or sleep in one of the lofts there. What begins, then, as a simple space ends up providing an admirable array of different places to be and things to do.

The architects assumed that in a vacation house choices of what to do and where to do it would be made casually, and so the feeling of the interior is relaxed. The details are simple, the rough-sawn boards are left unfinished, and the heavy framing members stand fully exposed.

Outside, this way of building produces an effect that is downright modest, recalling simple rural structures. It has turned out that, at the Sea Ranch, this assumption of modesty was wise, for as more and more houses are built on the open meadows, each more obviously "designed" than the next, and each one competing with all the others for attention, there is the danger that the place may begin to look more like a statuary farm than the beautifully desolate landscape which it once was, and which the original developers, planners and architects had sought with great care to preserve.

Architects: WILLIAM TURNBULL AND CHARLES MOORE of MLTW / Moore-Turnbull—Robert Theel, associate. *Location:* The Sea Ranch, California. *Engineers:* Patrick Morreau (structural); Brelje and Race (civil). *Contractor:* Matthew D. Sylvia.

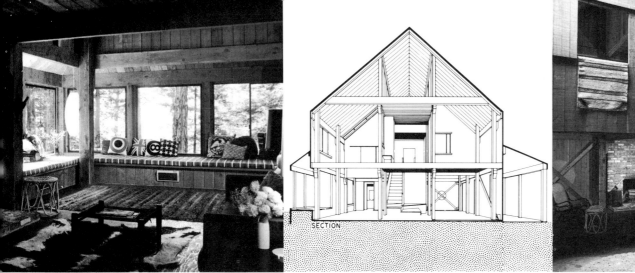

LOFT

SECOND FLOOR

FIRST FLOOR

Sharp-edged angularity for a San Francisco house

Remo Pratini photos except as noted

Edmund Burger

Patricia Coplans' hillside house in San Francisco rises in a conspiracy of angled planes and projections to overlook Golden Gate Park and the Pacific Ocean. The projecting bay windows are part of a local residential tradition but the sloping window walls (photos right) are a direct response to particular site conditions and the architect-owner's desire to capture as much sunlight as possible on this steeply contoured north slope.

The plan is compact and simply ordered in spite of the visual complications created by the pro-jections. The living room occupies the north end of the house over the garage and is overlooked, in turn, by a gallery level guest bedroom. Master bedroom and bath occupy the second floor over the kitchen. The sloping glass roof of the dining area frames a view up the slope of tall stands of eucalyptus. A central entry hall, also skylighted, is reached from the garage below or by a winding outdoor stair on the west side of the house.

Finish materials are sympa-thetically selected and detailed with skill. Exterior walls are West-ern Cedar nailed up in diagonals that echo the slope of the site in two directions. Interior partitions are gypsum board over wood studs; flooring is teak parquet for the living room and clay tile for dining room and kitchen. Rich accents, like the marble fireplace surround, are used sparingly. A dark red baked enamel finish, used on all gutters, down-spouts, window sash corner details and roof, contrasts warmly with the cedar siding, and gives the house a crisp, firm-edged angularity. This linear emphasis is restated inside in the window and door trim as in the unusually crisp and elegant sky-light details.

The Coplans house is invested with a stimulating spatial charac-ter—a character that is personal but not aberrant, a character that does not dissolve with the second or third look.

Architect and *owner:* PATRICIA A. COPLANS of Burger and Coplans. *Location:* San Francisco, Califor-nia. *Engineers:* Geoffrey Barrett (structural); James Peterson (me-chanical). *General contractor:* Pa-tricia Coplans.

The furnishings in the Coplans' house are a mixture of built-ins and modern classics in chrome, cane and leather. The relative formality of many of these pieces is surprising but no problems of compatability seem to arise.

Large skylights in many spaces flood the house with light but glazing is tinted for protection against the sun's direct rays.

Edmund Burger

Unexpected spaces formed by stretched fabric create a world of sensuous delight

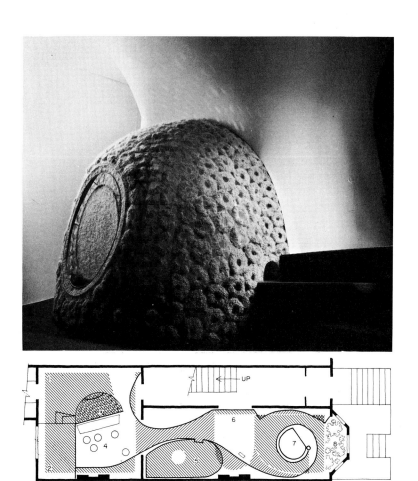

1 Work area	5 Group shelter	——— FLOOR PLAN
2 Writing	6 Entry	\\\\\\\\ STRETCH NYLON
3 Sleeping	7 Sensory	
4 Dining	8 Greenery	

Nathaniel Lieberman /Todd Watts photos

The parlor floor of the brownstone in which her sculptor husband, Vytautas, and she have worked for many years, seemed to Aleksandra Kasuba the perfect place for an experiment in sculpture for living. Two or three small-scale "environments" using stretched nylon fabric had convinced her of the potential visual delight of curved surfaces. But the execution of this project with eight separate areas, (plan left), has exceeded even her expectations. Relying heavily on her husband for technical advice and criticism, Mrs. Kasuba has developed joints at floor and ceiling, as well as around openings, (below), that effectively heighten the fabric's natural qualities rather than inhibit them. Lighting and light switches are so well integrated that one must know exactly where they are to find them. Beginning at the bay window filled with plants, (right), spaces unfold both as distinct shelters and as intertwining elements. Thus the view, from the entrance to the sensory, (an "individual shelter"), past the group shelter leads toward the eating area through a constantly changing tube of space. As one passes the group shelter, (below), he can see through the opening (and through the fabric to some extent) the opulent three-dimensional rug, (below left). Around behind the couch and movable tables is another surprise, the hemispherical sleeping bower of wovern yak hair on bent acrylic support strips (above left).

David Hirsch photos

Sound planning and simple detail rejuvenate a Manhattan brownstone

The usual deficiencies of New York brownstones—narrow width and dark interiors—were present when owner-architect Peter Samton and his wife began renovating. They had a tight budget but wanted openness, daylight and as much flexibility in spatial and furniture arrangements as possible.

The width was fixed at 16'-2" by the enclosing party walls. The street elevation was established at the building line. But by demolishing a small existing extension of the building at the rear, and by substituting a generous window wall, natural light could reach deep into the waist of the building. Living spaces are therefore defined by furniture groupings rather than transverse walls.

Living room, kitchen, dining and work spaces occupy the parlor floor; sleeping quarters and playroom are below. A small, in-

timate court, at rear, extends the play space and furnishes a pleasant taste of outdoors. Completing this handsome renovation are two rental apartments above.

Renovated Town House, New York City. Architect: *Peter Samton* (partner, *Gruzen & Partners*). Mechanical engineer: *Robert Freudenberg.*

In addition to flooding the main floor with light from the new green-house-like window wall, architect Peter Samton has added to the bright spaciousness of his renovated brownstone by a number of simple, but effective devices: creating a completely open plan with different "room" areas defined by low cabinets; using the same flooring throughout; exposing the original brick walls; and the selection of light, well-scaled furniture.

UPPER FLOOR   5   LOWER FLOOR

INDEX